PEARSON   ALWAYS LEARNING

Dr. Kenneth Forman • Dr. Wafa Deeb-Westervelt

Diving into Data
The key to improving instruction for 21st century education leaders

Custom Edition

D0139023

Pearson Education, Inc., 330 Hudson Street, New York, New York 10013
A Pearson Education Company
www.pearsoned.com

Printed in the United States of America

0002000102720125809

RM

ISBN 10: 1-323-43618-9
ISBN 13: 978-1-323-43618-9

25 2022

Diving into Data

...
The key to improving instruction for
21st century education leaders

Acknowledgements

We gratefully acknowledge the assistance of Stony Brook Educational Leadership faculty: Andrew Greene, Terrance O'Connor, Lynn Pombonyo, Stanley Kaminsky, Jeffrey Soloff and Robert Moraghan, Stony Brook EDL department chair, who took time from their busy schedules to serve as reviewers, giving us valuable feedback. We appreciate their productive conversations that helped facilitate the direction our book has taken. We are indebted to them for their guidance and support in getting this book to press and its use in the Stony Brook Educational Leadership Program.

Ken and Wafa

Personally, I wish to thank my wife for her patience and understanding for the time I spent at my computer in writing this book. You see it wasn't computer games...it was actually real work!

Ken

I would like to express my gratitude to my husband, Wayne, for his endless support and patience as I take on one project after the other. His wonderful sense of humor continues to serve me well, especially during moments of writer's block.

To Ken for reaching out to me to co-write this book with him. His perseverance and willingness to share in this project have, once again, stimulated my creativity and passion for writing.

Wafa

Table of Contents

Developing a Data-Driven Culture

A recent A T & T commercial claimed that, "Everyone loves data." Although this may be true when it comes to monitoring our cellular data usage, this sentiment does not necessarily hold true for educators. Data to educators is what garlic is to vampires. In order for schools to improve efforts in achieving higher academic standards, successful school leaders and teachers must continuously evaluate and monitor a variety of data sources (Smith, Johnson, & Thompson, 2012). However, past practice has placed accountability for student achievement on school districts rather than on individual schools (Oberman, Arbeit, Praglin, & Goldstein, 2005), while government interventions into state administered education programs, such as the No Child Left Behind (NCLB) and Race to the Top (RttT) initiatives have forced districts to re-examine student progress and ensure that all students achieve at designated benchmarks (Bernhardt, 2015). The increased emphasis on individual student achievement along with closing the achievement gap has caused districts to examine more closely the results of the state assessments and use that information to make decisions on forward progress (Datnow, Park, & Wohlstetter, 2007). Accordingly, the review of data became focused predominantly on state test results.

Data-driven decision-making has been universally defined to include analyses of data collected through various sources and the use of those findings to make informed decisions about instructional practices. Bernhardt (2015 & 2009) stated that if a school wants to improve student learning, it has to use data, while McQuiggan & Sapp (2014) posit that learning organizations cannot continue to make decisions without creating a culture of data. The research indicates that data-driven decision-making is a cyclical process based on inquiry with analysis giving educators new viable information to apply changes and new learning to the next cycle (Abbott & McKnight, 2010). As a result, the process of data-driven decision-making is not seen as a one-time event (Ikemoto & Marsh, 2007). Likewise, when school leaders successfully implement ongoing data-driven decision-making, those schools seek an increase in achievement levels and their staffs' ability to use and apply data to improve instruction (Bernhardt, 2009).

The focus on state testing results negates many variables that often contribute to student performance and, therefore, provide little input for educators to make informed decisions about their students. Teachers are unable to use summative assessments in a timely manner to provide feedback on student progress, address student weaknesses, or correct student misconceptions (Hattie, 2015; Heritage & Yeagley, 2005). As a result, teachers and administrators tend to view the use of data as of little importance to making informed decisions regarding instruction.

Conversely, data from formative assessments allow teachers to plan and alter instruction as the information can be used to highlight students' strengths and weaknesses (Datnow, et.al, 2007; Fuglei, 2014; Halverson, Prichett, & Watson, 2007). Moreover, data can also lead to understanding the causes or reasons for why students may not be progressing (Heritage, et.al, 2005). Relying on information gained from formative assessments will better enable teachers to address their students' areas in need of remediation and provide enrichment to those who may have met identified standards or grade-level expectations (Leahy, Lyon, Thompson, & William, 2005). Formative data include benchmark assessments, in-class assignments, teacher-created tests, homework assignments, anecdotal records, projects, and reports (Mandinach et.al, 2006). Most teachers continuously look at these types of data to evaluate student progress. Other types of data including student attendance, report card grades, benchmark assessments, and project-based activities (Heritage, et.al, 2005) can also help to shed light for teachers on their students' progress. Reviewing student work is an easy and readily accessible source of data to inform future instruction (Kazemi & Frankie, 2003; Tomlinson, 2015). With a variety of data sources, teachers can more accurately make decisions about student progress and identified areas of focus that they need to address in instruction (Halverson, et.al, 2007; Tomlinson, 2015).

Despite the fact that the need for district and school leaders to utilize data to inform instruction has never been greater, we still find many districts and schools that rely upon data for reporting purposes only. In other words, data use is viewed as a compliance issue rather than one that can inform instructional decision-making. To move from compliance to improvement, however, Bernhardt (2015) suggested that schools develop and implement a framework of continuous school improvement that focuses on the use of data to drive instructional practices. Deeb-Westervelt & Thompson (2010) identified a three-step framework aligned to Davenport's (1997) human-centered approach to information management in which he distinguished the constructs of data, information, and knowledge. The diagram below illustrates the hierarchical framework that leads teachers to transfer data into information and, ultimately, into knowledge about their students.

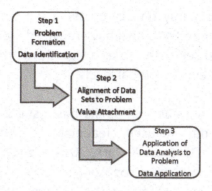

A Wisconsin school district utilizes 90-day action plans focused on evidence derived from data to improve instruction in their model (Sternke, 2016). Regardless of the framework, one of the roadblocks that must first be overcome is that many educators tend to review aggregated rather than disaggregated data in order to get to the root causes of issues. For example, superintendents, principals, teachers, and perhaps parents may compile the percentages of students who attained or exceeded proficiency levels on state-mandated assessments and draw conclusions from these numbers but often do not break down the data, especially data pertaining to the lack of student achievement. As a result, student achievement is viewed as a one-time event rather than a continuous feedback cycle that can assist in identifying the underlying factors that contributed to the results.

Many reasons contribute to educators' lack of willingness or desire to use data for instructional improvement. For example, despite the fact that the use of data to compare and contrast teachers is contrary to the school improvement movement, many states have implemented such models in response to the Race to the Top initiative. This has resulted in data use being viewed as a punitive rather than supportive measure. Coupled with statistically inadequate teacher and principal evaluation systems that are based primarily on aggregated state test results for students, fear and paranoia have replaced most educators' willingness to see data use as a viable practice for helping students achieve at optimal levels.

While high-stakes accountability has resulted in a greater need for data-focused leadership within learning organizations (Datnow & Park, 2014; Deeb-Westervelt & Thompson, 2010) and recognizing that the effective use of data can be a moving force within a school or district, many educational leaders still do not intentionally work toward creating effective data-driven learning organizations. Such organizations, however, are not only possible but are paramount, especially given that many school leaders utilize both quantitative and qualitative information gathered from both inside and outside of the classrooms to make daily decisions. Developing a data-driven culture requires first creating collaborative relationships between and among school leaders and teachers with both taking active leadership roles within their schools and classrooms (Datnow & Park, 2014). Knowing that collaboration is an effective approach to implementing change, however, is not without its challenges. As noted by Datnow & Park (2014), some of the greatest challenges that school leaders face is establishing a culture that supports data use and building teachers' capacity to utilize data to influence instructional decision-making. Other obstacles to establishing a data-driven decision-making culture include that it takes energy, motivation, and resources, as well as major alterations to the typical system and culture that operate in schools (Halverson, et.al, 2007). An equally important challenge is time; school leaders need to be resourceful and find creative ways of allocating time to work with data (McAdamis, 2007). An added challenge is presented when those working toward creating a culture of data-driven decision-making do not themselves know how to appropriately use data to inform instruction. As a result, teacher frustration or distrust toward school leaders grows. Marsh emphasized that a significant challenge is creating a want to use data (Marsh, et.al, 2006) mentality. But, schools often do not know where to begin or what types of data to use in their process of using that information to make decisions (Lachat, et.al, 2004).

Gathering and examining data to improve decision-making can be a starting point to developing a culture and system of continuous improvement that places student learning at the forefront (Datnow, et.al, 2007). Data need to be readily accessible in a timely manner so that teachers can develop the ability to appropriately analyze information. Datnow reported that when establishing expectations for data usage, if teachers are able to access data without difficulty and in a timely manner, they are more likely to use that data (Datnow, et.al, 2007). Analytic ability needs to be distributed across teachers so that capacity is built within the school (Halverson, et.al, 2007). Marsh, et.al (2015) stated that, "teachers do not always know how to use these data in ways that lead to deep changes in instruction and often lack skills and knowledge to interpret results and develop solutions." Ikemoto, et.al (2007) concur and assert that it is often assumed that teachers are adept at understanding data, discussing data, and making data informed decisions; however, many are not. Teachers are not experts in data collection and analysis and therefore, need ongoing professional development so that they have confidence when transitioning towards a culture of data usage (Bernhardt, 2009). The authors hypothesize that creating professional learning communities can help support teachers in analyzing and transferring data information to change instruction. It is important to keep in mind that successful implementation of data-driven decision-making relies on the school's capacity to invest in its teachers through providing ongoing professional development and support to choose the right data, understand and discuss that data, and make appropriate instructional decisions.

Schmoker (2004) suggested a different approach, the creation of leadership teams that develop goals to address questions raised about student performance within their school. He asserts that the potential for a positive impact on student achievement is amplified when the process of analyzing, identifying, prioritizing, and addressing student learning is distributed throughout the staff. To increase the likelihood of success for the team, expectations need to be set that data will always be the driving force for decisions and school leaders need to be exemplars of this process. Abbott, et.al (2010) support Schmoker's leadership team approach for school leaders looking to move their schools to a data-driven organization by surrounding themselves with a leadership team.

An alternate approach involves a school having a data coach or data facilitator (Marsh, et.al, 2015) who takes the lead in assisting teachers' work with data. The data coach or facilitator can lead a data team or a collaborative group of teachers around the examination of data. The research on data teams suggests that for effective data analysis to occur, school leaders have to develop tools, processes, and protocols to help teachers and other staff to monitor progress (Datnow, et.al, 2007).

Data teams need clearly articulated purposes as well as specific guidance. Thus, when data teams commence their work, the conversations that take place are critical to moving schools toward becoming data-driven organizations. In these conversations, targeted questions could focus and facilitate the data-driven discussions.

Using multiple sources of data that include student performance as well as demographic information can shed light for data teams on what is happening within individual classrooms as well as the school at large. As previously mentioned, data teams are successful when trust is created between teachers and school leaders. It is the responsibility of school leaders to create a data-driven culture within their schools, conducive to data-driven decision-making.

In Appendix A, we provide sample questions that might be used during data team meetings. Some of the questions can also be shared with individual teachers during pre- and/or post-observation conferences.

Whether using leadership or data teams, professional learning communities, or a data coach/facilitator, data-driven decision-making cannot be fully maximized to its greatest potential without the use of a data management system (Boudett, et.al, 2005). It is common that schools/districts have a great advantage in using a "data warehouse" which compiles information and provides access to data in order to make appropriate educational decisions. This affords district/school leaders, as well as the individual teachers opportunities to evaluate their students' strengths and weaknesses in order to improve instruction.

Marsh (2006) identified the following nine factors that influence the use of data for decision-making, many of which were previously discussed:

- accessibility of data;
- quality of data (real or perceived);
- motivation to use data;
- timeliness of data;

- staff capacity and support;
- curriculum pacing pressures;
- lack of time;
- organizational culture and leadership; and
- history of state accountability.

Data-driven decision-making and instructional leadership go hand-in-hand in order for improvement that schools and districts are striving for to take place (Creighton, 2001). Successful data-driven decision-making needs to facilitate a positive school culture of continuous inquiry and collaborative staff interaction to inform decisions, all with the intent of increasing student achievement (Boudett, et.al, 2005). Teachers need to have trust in each other and in their school leadership that the analysis of data is not meant to blame anyone for failures but rather to address weaknesses together (Datnow, et.al, 2007). In support of successful data-driven decision-making, schools must evidence a cultural shift that encourages the use and analysis of data without fear of reprisal (Marsh, et.al, 2006).

Two main components for successful data-driven decision-making include: measurable goals (school, teacher, and student) and a system-wide curriculum. A systemic curriculum with common benchmark assessments in place allows teachers to discuss student data together (Datnow, et.al, 2007).

Marsh, et.al (2006) also recommended the following leadership strategies (Appendix B) that facilitate the use of data and serve as focal points in the scenarios and discussion points presented in the subsequent pages of this book:

- Establishing a clear vision for the use of data;
- Providing supports that promote a data-driven environment;
- Making data an ongoing part of the improvement process;
- Creating a process or structure to analyze data;
- Teaching students to examine their own data;
- Providing professional development on what the data tell you and how to use that information;
- Facilitating an organizational culture that supports data use for continuous improvement; and
- Providing teacher/data coach leadership.

We believe that if the use of data were to be seen as a strategy to identify and amplify areas of excellence and/or to remediate areas for improvement, districts and schools would be better able to enhance teaching and learning for all students. As a result, the performance tasks in this book utilize Marsh's strategies for creating data-driven cultures. Consequently, the purposes of this book are to enable educators to gain a deeper understanding of data-driven decision-making, how this process can be implemented effectively through best practices, and recognize whether or not improvements in student performance are noted as a result. Because school and district leaders need to make informed decisions in an ongoing basis and usually in rapid-fire succession, this book provides the reader opportunities to practice decision-making skills using data provided in varied scenarios, while also identifying the challenges associated with moving to a data-driven model. The included scenarios require the reader to review, analyze, and interpret data in order to gain a deeper understanding of factors contributing to organizational effectiveness. These scenarios can be utilized for professional development opportunities by leaders with teachers so that they, too, can gain more confidence in their abilities to use data to guide decisions about their students. We encourage the creation of data teams within schools when moving towards a data-driven model for decision-making. As noted earlier, data teams offer a collaborative approach between leaders and their teachers and, therefore, help empower teachers to take the lead in change and improvement processes. As a result, teachers will take on teacher leader roles and facilitate the use of data for academic improvement. Concomitantly, this book is also intended to more fully prepare prospective school leaders for the required exams to become certified as School Building Leader (SBL) or School District Leader (SDL).

In an earlier part of this book, we made an argument for the importance of using formative data to drive decisions. However, the data presented in the scenarios are based on summative state assessments which are used by the state for statistical analyses and school effectiveness ratings. As a result, we decided to mirror this format in our book to more fully prepare prospective administrators for licensing examinations. Nevertheless, practicing school leaders should rely on both formative and summative assessment data and multiple sources of data when creating data-driven cultures.

If you are using this book as part of test preparation for the New York State School Building Leader (SBL) and/or School District Leader (SDL) examinations, read each scenario and then answer each question on your computer as if you were under "testing" conditions. Although the examinations do not allocate a specific time to each question, it is recommended that you spend about 60 minutes responding to the performance task at the end of each scenario. Understand that being successful on any written examination requires the examinee to rapidly and accurately size up a problem, using sound judgment to resolve each data-driven scenario. A solution and a rationale for responding to each question are provided separately in the back of the book. Solutions represent a logical resolution based upon our experiences as school and district leaders. There can also be varying viewpoints as long as they are supported by the presented data. Questions for our scenarios (performance tasks) have been taken from the New York State Teacher Certification Examination website (NYSTCE), School Building Leader Examination page. All responses have been validated and field tested.

Diving into Data is in alignment with the 2015 Professional Standards for Educational Leaders (Appendix C), as developed by the National Policy Board for Educational Administration. (Appendix C) "These standards are organized around the domains, qualities and values of leadership work that research and practice indicate contribute to students' academic success and well-being" (Professional Standards, 2015).

Performance Task 1

1. What are two primary issues presented in this scenario, and why do you believe this to be so?

2. What are two important questions you must address in order to explore this issue? Explain why each is important to address.

3. How will you go about getting answers to each question? What challenges might you face in getting answers to your questions?

4. Describe one possible finding of your inquiry process and the potential action that finding would imply.

Performance Task 2

1. Identify one strength of this school, citing evidence to support your response.

2. Identify three areas of need in the instructional program, citing evidence to support each need.

3. Which area of need would be your highest priority? Explain.

4. What are two important questions you must answer to address your highest priority area of need? Explain why each question is important to address. *Must relate to Q3.*

5. How will you go about getting answers to EACH question?

6. What actions would you take to address the school's priority need? Explain why. *Refer to Q3.*

7. How would you leverage the identified strength of the school to address the priority need? *Refer to Q1.*

8. What possible challenges might your actions create and what are some ways that you could manage these challenges? *Refer to Q6.*

Alpha Junior High School

Courtesy of Jesse Kunerth. Shutterstock

983 Students
65 Teachers

Alpha Junior High School

Alpha Junior High School is a school located in a blue collar middle class suburban community. It includes 983 students in grades seven and eight from a variety of ethnic backgrounds. You are the newly assigned principal and are assisted by two assistant principals. There are 65 teachers on staff, most of whom have been teaching at the school for more than five years. In reviewing the school's data, you identify issues with student achievement that you must address. A particular area of concern for the principal is the equitable representation of all student subgroups in the school's gifted program.

Discussion
Let's review the leadership characteristics and strategies used to facilitate the use of data at the school:
- Establishing a clear vision for the use of data:
  The school building leader recognizes a need to review the data especially in the gifted program. However, neither the assistant principals nor teachers are recognized as participants in any review process.
- Providing supports that promote a data-driven environment:
  The scenario does not include any structures that have been put into place for reviewing data.
- Making data an ongoing part of the improvement process:
  The scenario does not include any mechanism for any data review process.
- Creating a process or structure to analyze data: In the scenario, the principal has neither established processes nor structures within the organization to regularly review achievement data.

- Teaching students to examine their own data: Likewise, the scenario provides no structures for students to become cognizant of their achievement including developing next steps for improvement.
- Providing professional development on what the data tells you and how to use it:
  The scenario provides no indication that ongoing professional development is taking place based upon analysis of data.
- Facilitating an organizational culture that supports data use for continuous improvement:
  There is no ongoing professional development that might encourage teachers to analyze their own data. Table 1 indicates that the majority of the teachers are highly experienced (62% of teachers have a Master's Degree+30 credits). There are no teachers not highly qualified and no teachers are teaching out of license.
- Providing teacher/data coach leadership:
  Having such an experienced staff lends itself to creating teacher leadership opportunities as data coaches, teacher trainers or teacher leaders. The scenario indicates that there are no structures like these evident in the organization.

Table 1: Staffing

Principal	1
Assistant Principal	2
Total teachers	65
Teacher turnover rate	6%
Percent teachers teaching out of license	0
Percent teachers with less than 3 years	2%
Percent teachers with Master's + 30	62%
Percent teachers not highly qualified	0

Table 2: Alpha School Demographics

Black	Hispanic	Asian	White	Total	LEP	SWD	Suspensions	Attendance	Free/ Red. Lunch
390	297	178	115	983	9	109	89		226
40%	30%	18%	12%		1%	11%	9%	97%	27%
Gifted and Talented Program Participation									
6%	10%	28%	56%	147	1%	8%			

Table 3a: Grade 7 English Language Arts Achievement

	Current Year % scoring at level:					Last Year % scoring at level:				
	1	2	3	4	3+4	1	2	3	4	3+4
Statewide	32	37	23	8	31	8	39	49	4	51
All Students	16	43	28	14	42	3	28	66	3	69
Gen Education	11	44	31	15	46	1	25	70	4	74
SWD	60	34	6	0	6	22	65	13	0	13
Asian	13	29	37	21	58	0	22	73	5	78
Black	14	41	30	15	45	2	34	63	1	64
Hispanic	20	51	21	8	29	5	25	65	5	70
Poverty	19	47	26	8	34	5	34	59	1	60
Non Poverty	15	41	29	16	45	2	26	68	4	72

Table 3b: Grade 7 Mathematics Achievement

	Current Year % scoring at level:					Last Year % scoring at level:				
	1	2	3	4	3+4	1	2	3	4	3+4
Statewide	38	34	20	7	27	9	26	34	31	65
All Students	28	40	28	4	32	4	19	43	33	76
Gen Education	21	43	31	5	36	2	18	45	35	80
SWD	83	14	3	0	3	30	39	22	9	31
Asian	15	34	39	13	52	0	12	40	48	88
Black	33	35	29	3	32	3	23	51	23	74
Hispanic	26	52	20	2	22	6	19	43	33	76
Poverty	36	42	18	4	22	5	20	43	32	75
Non Poverty	24	39	32	4	36	3	19	44	34	78

Table 4a: Grade 8 English Language Arts Achievement

	Current Year % scoring at level:					Last Year % scoring at level:				
	1	2	3	4	3+4	1	2	3	4	3+4
Statewide	30	37	23	10	33	7	42	48	2	50
All Students	12	37	34	17	51	3	39	55	2	57
Gen Education	6	38	38	18	56	2	35	61	2	63
SWD	68	29	3	0	3	17	69	14	0	14
Asian	7	35	43	15	58	2	29	65	4	69
Black	13	43	33	11	44	4	43	52	1	53
Hispanic	12	34	34	20	54	2	51	47	0	47
Poverty	20	32	37	11	48	5	46	47	1	48
Non Poverty	10	38	33	19	52	3	37	58	2	60

Table 5: Grade 8 Mathematics Achievement

	Current Year % scoring at level:					Last Year % scoring at level:				
	1	2	3	4	3+4	1	2	3	4	3+4
Statewide	31	41	20	7	27	7	31	42	20	62
All students	22	56	21	2	23	4	24	53	19	72
Gen Education	16	60	23	2	25	2	21	56	21	77
SWD	84	16	0	0	0	24	50	26	0	26
Asian	8	60	27	5	32	2	15	62	22	84
Black	27	61	12	1	13	5	29	55	11	66
Hispanic	23	54	22	0	22	6	26	48	20	68
Poverty	32	50	17	1	18	7	33	46	. 14	60
Non Poverty	19	57	22	2	24	3	21	55	20	75

Table 6: Middle Level English Language Arts and Mathematics Results for Accountability Adequate Yearly Progress (AYP) – Current Year

	English Language Arts		Mathematics	
	Made AYP	Tested 95%	Made AYP	Tested 95%
All Students	✓	✓	✓	✓
SWD	✓	✓	X	✓
Asian	✓	✓	✓	✓
Black	✓	✓	✓	✓
Hispanic	✓	✓	✓	✓
White	✓	✓	✓	✓
Poverty	✓	✓	✓	✓

X=subgroup did not make AYP

Selected Response:
1. Based on the data preceding scenario, the most pressing issue for Alpha Junior High School is:
   A. Improved performance of the Hispanic subgroup.
   B. Underperformance of the SWDs subgroup.

C. Performance of the All Students subgroup above the statewide average on the 8th grade English Language Arts assessment.
D. Consistent performance of the Asian subgroup above the statewide average in English Language Arts and Mathematics.

2. In looking at Table 6, Middle Level English Language Arts and Mathematics Results for Accountability Adequate Yearly Progress, which subgroup did not make Adequate Yearly Progress for either English Language Arts or Mathematics?
  A. SWDs
  B. Asian
  C. Black
  D. Poverty

3. In examining the staffing at Alpha Junior High School, which of the following statements is correct?
  A. 10% of the teachers are not highly qualified.
  B. 38% of the teachers do not have a Master's Degree + 30 credits.
  C. 5 teachers have less than 3 years' experience.
  D. 2% of the teachers are teaching out of license.

4. The principal reviewed the school demographic data (Table 2) and found the following:
  A. 88% of the population is minority
  B. The representation of LEP students in the Gifted program is consistent with the school's demographics for this subgroup.
  C. There is an overrepresentation of Hispanic students in the Gifted Program.
  D. Student attendance is above 95%

23

Performance Task:

1. Give one strength of Alpha Junior High School. What evidence would you use to support this determination? What strategy might you use to enhance this strength?

2. List three areas of need for Alpha Junior High School. What evidence would you use to support this determination?

3. Which area of need would be your highest priority? Explain why.

4. What are two important questions you must answer to address your highest priority? Explain why each question is important to address.

5. How would you go about getting answers to each question?

6. What actions would you take to address the school's priority need? Explain why.

7. How would you leverage the identified strength of the school to address the priority need?

8. What possible challenges might your actions create and what are some ways that you could manage these challenges?

Bravo Academy

Courtesy of Jörg Carstensen. Pearson Education Ltd

1410 Students
79 Teachers

Bravo Academy

Bravo Academy is a grades K-5 elementary school located in a blue collar multi-ethnic community within an urban area. The school consists of 1410 students from a variety of ethnic backgrounds. You have been principal at this school for four years and you are assisted by four assistant principals. You have established a school management committee and a data subcommittee consisting of school leaders, teachers and parents. There are 79 teachers on staff with a small number of them (11), teaching less than three years. The school's data committee has examined the school's achievement data, concluding that there are some academic issues.

Discussion
The leadership characteristics and strategies used to facilitate the use of data at this school include:
- Establishing a clear vision for the use of data:
  The principal at Bravo Academy has established a vision for using data by implementing structures that involve teachers in data analysis. The management team and the data committee are both structures that emphasize teacher participation in the use of data.
- Providing supports that promote a data-driven environment:
  The principal and the four assistant principals have encouraged teacher participation via school management and data analysis teams.
- Making data an ongoing part of the improvement process:
  Bravo Academy has made the analysis part of the improvement process by establishing a data committee.

- Creating a process or structure to analyze data: The data committee includes school leaders, teachers and parents and is charged with examining student achievement data and making suggestions to the school management committee for instructional improvement.
- Teaching students to examine their own data: There are no structures evident that support students having opportunities to examine their own data.
- Providing professional development on what the data tells you and how to use it:
  Although not specifically mentioned in the narrative, the implication that a data committee is examining the achievement data and reporting back to the school management committee implies action to be taken regarding that information. In providing the school management committee findings regarding the analysis of data, the next logical step would include professional development in teaching and learning based upon those findings.
- Facilitating an organizational culture that supports data use for continuous improvement:
  This school promotes a positive culture by involving teachers in leadership opportunities in school management and data analysis.
- Providing teacher/data coach leadership: Although there is a school governance committee and data analysis committee in place, there is no indication of any teacher leader or data coach on staff. However, shared decision-making implies the potential to involve teachers in leadership opportunities.

Table 1: Staffing

Principal	1
Assistant Principal	4
Total teachers	79
Teacher turnover rate	9%
Teachers teaching out of license	1
Teachers with less than 3 years	11/13%
Teachers with Master's + 30	55/70%
Percent teachers not highly qualified	0
Ineffective rating (number/%)	0/0%
Developing rating (number/%)	2/3%
Effective rating (number/%)	58/73%
Highly Effective rating (number/%)	19/24%

Table 2: Student Demographics

Total Pop.	Black	Hispanic	Asian	White	ELL	SWD	Suspensions	Attend.	Free/Red Lunch
	8%	28%	60%	4%	4%	14%		94%	86%
1410	112	396	839	63	63	204	4		1207

Table 3: English Language Arts Achievement

	Grade 3: % scoring at level:					Grade 4: % scoring at level:					Grade 5: % scoring at level:				
	1	2	3	4	3+4	1	2	3	4	3+4	1	2	3	4	3+4
Statewide	32	37	22	9	31	31	37	23	10	33	36	36	20	9	29
All Students	18	39	29	15	44	11	45	26	18	44	24	39	19	18	37
Gen Education	15	38	25	22	47	9	42	29	20	49	18	41	21	20	41
SWD	48	42	8	2	10	23	60	14	3	17	62	27	8	4	12
Asian	15	37	30	17	47	9	41	27	23	50	21	39	21	19	40
Black	15	38	30	17	47	4	43	35	17	52	18	27	18	36	54
Hispanic	22	44	26	8	34	15	54	25	6	31	29	45	16	11	27
Poverty	19	41	28	12	40	12	48	26	14	40	24	40	21	14	35

Table 4: Mathematics Achievement

	Grade 3: % scoring at level					Grade 4: % scoring at level:					Grade 5: % scoring at level:				
	1	2	3	4	3+4	1	2	3	4	3+4	1	2	3	4	3+4
Statewide	31	33	24	14	36	27	31	24	18	42	32	29	24	15	39
All Students	19	38	24	19	43	11	34	28	27	55	11	27	29	32	61
Gen Education	13	38	32	17	49	7	35	28	30	58	9	27	30	34	64
SWD	53	32	12	3	15	31	29	31	9	40	31	31	23	15	38
Asian	15	35	26	24	50	8	32	25	35	60	10	24	32	34	66
Black	17	35	28	20	48	9	26	48	17	65	9	36	18	36	54
Hispanic	28	45	17	10	27	16	44	26	14	40	14	33	26	26	52
Poverty	21	40	23	17	40	12	36	27	25	52	12	29	29	29	58

Table 5: Accountability - Adequate Yearly Progress (AYP) for Participation

	English Language Arts			Mathematics		
	Made AYP	95% Tested	Safe Harbor	Made AYP	95% Tested	Safe Harbor
All Students	YES	YES	YES	YES	YES	YES
Asian	YES	YES	YES	YES	YES	YES
Black	YES	YES	YES	YES	YES	YES
Hispanic	YES	YES	YES	YES	YES	YES
SWD	NO	YES	NO	NO	YES	NO
Free/Red . Lunch	YES	YES	YES	YES	YES	YES

Selected Response:

1. As principal of the Bravo Academy, after reviewing the data about your school, what would be a pressing issue you would identify?

    A. The percent of SWDs functioning at Levels 3 & 4 on English Language Arts and Mathematics Assessments.

    B. Low performance, at Levels 3 & 4, for Asians on English Language Arts and Mathematics assessments.

    C. The high rate of suspensions over the current school year.

    D. The high rate of teacher turnover.

2. In looking carefully at the English Language Arts assessment the principal determined:

    A. SWDs in grades 3, 4, & 5 scored above the statewide average as evidenced by their Level 3+4 scores.

    B. Those in the All Student subgroup in grades 3, 4 & 5 performed consistently above the statewide average as evidenced by their Level 3+4 scores.

C. Students identified as "Poverty" scored below the statewide average as evidenced by their Level 3+4 scores.

D. The highest scoring subgroup identified in Table 3 was Asian.

3. In looking carefully at Table 4 for this school, the principal confirmed all the following were correct, except:

A. All Students performed consistently above the statewide average.

B. Levels 3+4 performance of the General Education population exceeded that of the Statewide population for English Language Arts and Mathematics.

C. Students with Disabilities (SWDs) Mathematics scored in Levels 1 and 2 were higher than scores for Levels 3+4 across all grades.

D. The Asian subgroup performed consistently lower in Levels 3+4 across all grades.

4. Looking at Table 5, Accountability Results for Bravo Academy, which of the following statements is incorrect:

A. The Hispanic subgroup attained Adequate Yearly Progress.

B. The Free/Reduced Lunch subgroup attained Adequate Yearly Progress.

C. The Black subgroup attained Adequate Yearly Progress.

D. All subgroups attained Adequate Yearly Progress.

Performance Task:

1. What are two primary issues presented by the data and why do you believe it to be so? Two primary issues presented by the data:

2. What are two important questions you must address as principal to explore this issue? Explain why each question is important?

3. How will you go about getting answers to each question? What challenges might you face in getting answers to your questions?

4. Describe one possible finding of your inquiry process and the potential action that finding would imply.

Charlie High School

Courtesy of Cynthia Farmer. Shutterstock

Dr. Fitz, Principal
929 Students
86 Teachers

Charlie High School

Charlie High School is located in a blue collar community within a surrounding suburban area. It has 929 students in grades 9-12 coming from a variety of ethnic backgrounds. However, the school's population is decreasing. The principal, Dr. Fitz, is tenured and has served as school building leader for fifteen years. Dr. Fitz believes that the administrative team makes the decisions and shares them with the teachers. The principal is assisted by two assistant principals, one of which is tenured and the other newly appointed. The newly appointed assistant principal has been charged by the superintendent with establishing a school management team including varying constituencies to examine the school's academic performance and create a more data-driven environment. There are 86 teachers on staff, mostly senior teachers, rated effective or highly effective. However, the superintendent has indicated that Charlie High School has a number of issues.

Discussion
The leadership characteristics and strategies used to facilitate the use of data at the school include:
- Establishing a clear vision for the use of data:
  The principal doesn't express a clear vision for the shared use of data; his expectation is that only he and his assistant principals have the efficacy to use data to look at performance.
- Providing supports that promote a data-driven environment:
  The only support provided is that the high school has two assistant principals who along with the principal account for the school's data analysis.
- Making data an ongoing part of the improvement process:

The superintendent has expressed the desire to create a data-driven culture at Charlie High School by charging the newly appointed assistant principal with the responsibility of creating a school management team, the first step towards a data-driven environment. However, this charge is without the principal's acknowledgement.

- Creating a process or structure to analyze data:
  The principal has not expressed any will to create a mutually participative data-driven environment at his school. However, the superintendent has expressed a desire to change the school's culture implementing shared decision-making and establishing data-driven instruction.

- Teaching students to examine their own data:
  Without any teacher driven data structure in place, students are not able to examine their own data.

- Providing professional development on what the data tells you and how to use it:
  Professional development could support teachers, especially with the effort of the newly appointed assistant principal's charge to invigorate the use of data. However, there is no indication of any structures previously established to support teachers' development.

- Facilitating an organizational culture that supports data use for continuous improvement:
  With the principal's philosophy that the administrative team makes the decisions and shares them with the teachers, the culture mostly likely is negative. It appears that data is not an influential factor that supports academic achievement.

- Providing teacher/data coach leadership:
  The principal believes that his assistant principals are all the teachers need to coach them in use of

data. However, the superintendent has a different belief by engendering the creation of a school management team that could look at data to support instruction.

Table 1: Staffing

Principal	1
Assistant Principals	2
Total teachers	86
Teacher turnover rate	15%
Teachers teaching out of license	0
Percent teachers with less than 3 years	1%
Percent teachers with Master's + 30	58%
Percent teachers not highly qualified	0
Ineffective rating (number/%)	1/1%
Developing rating (number/%)	0/0
Effective rating (number/%)	59/69%
Highly Effective rating (number/%)	26/30%

Table 2: Student Demographics

Total Pop.	Black	Hispanic	Asian	White	ELL	SWD	Suspensions	Attend.	Free/Red Lunch
	26%	41%	7%	26%	5%	19%	7%	91%	51%
929	240	377	69	240	47	178	65		478

Table 3: High School Completers

	Graduates + IEP	Regents Diploma		Adv. Regents Diploma		Non-Completers	
		Number	%	Number	%	Number	%
All Students	209	175	85	59	29	30	3
Gen Education	173	167	97	58	34		
SWD	36	8	25	1	3		

36

Table 4: Post-Graduation Plans of Completers

	Four year college		Two year college		Military		Employment		Unknown	
	#	%	#	%	#	%	#	%	#	%
All Students	98	47	57	27	1	0	10	5	42	20
Gen Education	92	53	49	28	1	1	7	4	23	14
SWD	6	17	8	22	0	0	3	8	19	53

Table 5a: English Regents Examination Results

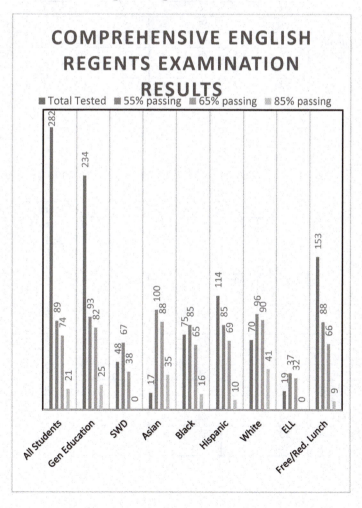

COMPREHENSIVE ENGLISH REGENTS EXAMINATION RESULTS

■ Total Tested ■ 55% passing ▨ 65% passing ▨ 85% passing

Table 5b: History Regents Examination Results

	Global History and Geography				US History and Government			
		(Percent of students scoring at or above)				(Percent of students scoring at or above)		
	Total Tested	55	65	85	Total Tested	55	65	85
All Students	316	72	57	25	278	88	77	36
Gen Education	257	79	66	30	236	89	81	39
SWD	59	44	20	2	42	81	57	14
Asian	18	--	--	--	2	--	--	--
Black	80	65	45	8	72	88	78	26
Hispanic	133	68	52	20	112	83	68	22
White	81	83	75	43	73	92	88	60
ELL	17	29	12	0	15	47	13	0
Free/Red. Lunch	174	67	49	15	142	88	82	46

Table 5c: Science Regents Examination Results

	Living Environment				Earth Science			
		(Percent of students scoring at or above)				(Percent of students scoring at or above)		
	Total Tested	55	65	85	Total Tested	55	65	85
All Students	217	89	64	7	287	78	53	13
Gen Education	172	94	73	9	231	84	60	15
SWD	45	71	27	0	56	55	23	2
Asian	14	--	--	--	17	--	--	--
Black	57	89	51	0	78	60	35	6
Hispanic	100	87	63	4	131	82	55	8
White	45	93	78	16	57	84	68	25
ELL	9	67	44	44	1	--	--	--
Free/Red. Lunch	130	86	57	5	169	75	49	8

Table 5d: Mathematics Regents Examination Results
Algebra I, Geometry, Algebra II/Trigonometry

	Algebra I				Geometry				Trigonometry			
	Total	55%	65%	85%	Total	55%	65%	85%	Total	55%	65%	85%
All Students	217	89	68	10	273	75	54	15	137	77	63	18
Gen Education	167	96	77	12	251	76	57	16	132	77	63	18
SWD	50	64	38	2	22	64	23	5	5	60	60	20
Asian	--	--	--	--	15	100	93	47	14	--	--	--
Black	64	83	58	3	58	67	47	5	32	72	53	9
Hispanic	105	92	73	14	118	70	47	10	48	69	50	8
White	34	91	65	6	76	86	64	25	42	86	79	31
ELL	204	89	68	10	2	--	--	--	0	0	0	0
Free/Red Lunch	140	86	69	10	149	71	47	10	58	62	45	5

Table 6: Accountability - Adequate Yearly Progress
(AYP) Participation

	English Language Arts				Mathematics			
	Made AYP	95% Tested	% 12th graders with valid scores	Safe Harbor	Made AYP	95% Tested	% 12th graders with valid scores	Safe Harbor
All Students	NO	YES	100	NO	NO	YES	100	NO
Asian	--	--	--	--	--	--	--	--
Black	NO	YES	100	NO	YES	YES	99	YES
Hispanic	YES	YES	100	YES	YES	YES	100	YES
White	YES	YES	100	YES	YES	YES	100	YES
SWD	NO	--	--	NO	NO	--	--	NO
ELL	--	--	--	--	--	--	--	--
Free/Red. Lunch	NO	YES	100	NO	NO	YES	99	NO

Table 7: Graduation Rate for Accountability (AYP)

	Overall Graduation Rate	Four Year Graduation Rate	Five Year Graduation Rate
	Made AYP?	Made AYP?	Made AYP?
All Students	YES	YES	YES
Asian	--	--	--
Black	YES	YES	NO
Hispanic	YES	NO	YES
White	YES	YES	YES
SWD	YES	YES	YES
ELL	--	--	--
Free/Red. Lunch	YES	YES	YES

Selected Response:

1. All of the following issues are pressing needs at Charlie High School, except:

> *A. Five year graduation rate for Black students.*
> *B. Adequate Yearly Progress for Students of Poverty (Free/Reduced Lunch).*
> *C. The percentage of graduating SWDs receiving Regents diplomas.*
> *D. The Four year graduation rate for Hispanic students.*

2. Looking at Tables 5c and 5d, Regents Examination Results, which statement is correct:

> *A. SWDs performed equally as well as all General Education students on all Regents examinations.*
> *B. The percentages of Hispanic students decreased when comparing achievement at 55%, 65%, and 85% on the Mathematics Regents examinations.*
> *C. The largest number of students completed the Trigonometry Regents.*
> *D. More students took the Living Environment Regents than the Earth Science Regents.*

3. In reviewing Table 3: High School Completers and Table 4: Post-Graduation Plans of Completers, which one of the following statements is NOT true:

    A. There were 30 non-high school completers.
    B. 74% of the students went on to either a two year or four year college.
    C. 61% of SWDs pursued higher education after completing high school.
    D. Less than 30% of the graduating SWDs received a Regents or Advanced Regents Diploma.

4. In examining the professional status of educators teaching at Charlie High School, all the following are true, except:

    A. 93% of the teachers were APPR rated Effective or Highly Effective.
    B. There is a large percentage of teachers not highly qualified.
    C. At least 51 teachers have a Master's Degree + 30 credits.
    D. There is a very small percentage of teachers teaching less than three years.

Performance Task:

1. Identify one strength of the school, citing evidence to support your response.

2. Identify three areas of need in the instructional program, citing evidence to support each need.

3. Which area of need would be your highest priority? Explain why.

4. *What are two important questions you must answer to address your highest priority? Explain why each question is important to address.*

5. *How will you go about getting answers to each question?*

6. *What actions would you take to address the school's priority need? Explain why.*

7. *How would you leverage the identified strength of the school to address the priority need?*

8. *What possible challenges might your actions create and what are some ways that you could manage these challenges?*

Delta Middle School

Courtesy of Cynthia Farmer. Shutterstock

Dr. Finger, Principal
981 Students
81 Teachers

Delta Middle School

Delta Middle School is a grade 6-8 school of distinction, located in a wealthy suburban community whose parents mostly commute to work in large metropolitan city. There are 981 students, with a small percentage of students from minority subgroups. The principal, Dr. Kenneth Finger, was appointed eight years ago; he is well-respected and liked by teachers, parents and students. Dr. Finger and his two assistant principals have established protocols to empower teachers to examine their students' achievement, including a teacher led data committee. The principal has provided time for the data committee to meet during the school day and has compensated members for their work on the committee. Committee members are required to share their findings with their colleagues. Although the school's report card evidences significant achievement, Dr. Finger and the data committee have identified a number of challenges.

Discussion

The leadership characteristics and strategies used to facilitate the use of data at the school include:

- Establishing a clear vision for the use of data:
  Delta Middle School is high achieving where school leaders and teachers collaboratively work together to use data to inform instruction as evidenced by the work of the school data committee.
- Providing supports that promote a data-driven environment:
  The principal and his assistant principals support a data-driven environment by providing the school data committee compensation for their extended work and time for meeting during the school day.
- Making data an ongoing part of the improvement process:

Data is an ongoing part of the improvement process as evidenced by the work of the data team and the school's high achievement in many academic areas above statewide averages.

- Creating a process or structure to analyze data: The teacher led school data committee is a structure used to analyze data at the school.
- Teaching students to examine their own data: There is no evidence to support that students' examine their own data.
- Providing professional development on what the data tells you and how to use it:
  As a result of a teacher led school data committee that has the responsibility of sharing their findings with colleagues, student achievement is beyond expectation for the All Students subgroup and most other subgroups. Collegial sharing provides support for professional development on use of data.
- Facilitating an organizational culture that supports data use for continuous improvement:
  With the establishment of the teacher led school data committee, a culture has been established that supports the use of data to inform instruction.
- Providing teacher/data coach leadership:
  There is no evidence to support the use of teacher leaders or data coaches except that members of the data committee are expected to share information and findings with their colleagues.

Table 1: Staffing

Principal	1
Assistant Principals	2
Total teachers	81
Teacher turnover rate	16%
Teachers teaching out of license	0
Percent teachers with less than 3 years	1%
Percent teachers with Master's + 30	75%
Percent teachers not highly qualified	0
Ineffective rating (number/%)	1/1%
Developing rating (number/%)	0/0
Effective rating (number/%)	30/37%
Highly Effective rating (number/%)	50/62%

Table 2: Student Demographics

Total Pop.	Black	Hispanic	Asian	White	ELL	SWD	Suspensions	Attend.	Free/Red Lunch
	12%	9%	12%	65%	1%	21%	1%	96%	16%
981	116	85	119	637	14	207	9		159

Table 3: English Language Arts Achievement

	Grade 6: % scoring at level:					Grade 7: % scoring at level:					Grade 8: % scoring at level:				
	1	2	3	4	3+4	1	2	3	4	3+4	1	2	3	4	3+4
Statewide	29	42	16	14	30	32	37	23	8	31	30	37	23	10	33
All Students	20	43	18	19	37	15	35	35	14	49	15	28	39	19	58
Gen Education	9	47	21	23	44	7	36	41	16	57	4	26	45	24	69
SWD	69	27	2	2	4	59	35	7	0	7	54	32	13	0	13
Asian	8	43	27	22	49	11	19	39	31	70	8	26	36	31	67
Black	24	52	16	8	24	34	34	17	15	32	31	34	23	11	34
Hispanic	47	32	21	0	21	23	35	38	4	42	24	27	30	18	48
White	18	44	16	22	38	11	39	38	12	50	11	27	43	19	62
Poverty	43	43	2	11	13	36	34	18	11	29	36	27	27	9	36

Table 4: Mathematics Achievement

	Grade 6: % scoring at level:					Grade 7: % scoring at level:					Grade 8: % scoring at level:				
	1	2	3	4	3+4	1	2	3	4	3+4	1	2	3	4	3+4
Statewide	29	41	18	12	30	38	34	20	7	27	31	41	20	7	27
All Students	14	36	24	27	51	14	24	40	22	62	15	43	37	5	42
Gen Education	5	37	27	32	59	6	23	45	26	71	3	42	49	6	55
SWD	58	30	9	2	11	53	30	14	2	16	39	46	14	2	16
Asian	5	22	32	41	73	3	11	34	51	86	0	62	31	8	39
Black	29	42	17	13	30	37	21	24	18	42	19	50	27	4	31
Hispanic	16	58	16	11	27	27	35	23	15	38	17	46	33	4	37
White	12	36	25	27	52	8	26	74	20	67	15	38	43	5	48
Poverty	37	39	11	13	24	32	36	25	7	32	19	44	31	6	37

Table 5: Science-Grade 8 vs. Science Regents Grade 8

	Science Grade 8 % scoring level:					Science Regents Grade 8 % scoring level:				
	1	2	3	4	3+4	1	2	3	4	3+4
Statewide	6	21	43	30	73					
All Students	1	15	47	37	84	0	0	6	94	100
Gen Education	0	4	46	50	96					
SWD	3	34	49	13	63					
Asian	0	0	67	33	100					
Black	4	24	52	20	72					
Hispanic	0	30	48	22	70					
White	1	11	43	45	88					
Poverty	0	22	53	24	77					

Table 6: Accountability - Adequate Yearly Progress (AYP)-Participation

	English Language Arts			Mathematics			Science		
	Made AYP	95% Tested	Safe Harbor	Made AYP	95% Tested	Safe Harbor	Made AYP	95% Tested	Safe Harbor
All Students	YES	YES	YES	NO	NO	YES	YES	YES	YES
Asian	YES	YES	YES	YES	YES	YES	YES	YES	YES
Black	YES	YES	YES	YES	YES	YES	YES	--	YES
Hispanic	YES	YES	YES	YES	YES	YES	YES	--	YES
White	YES	YES	YES	NO	NO	YES	YES	YES	YES
SWD	YES	YES	YES	NO	NO	YES	YES	YES	YES
ELL	--	--	--	--	--	--	--	--	--
Free/Red Lunch	YES	YES	YES	NO	NO	YES	YES	YES	YES

Selected Response:

1. Dr. Finger, principal at Delta Middle School identified all the following as the strengths, except:
   - A. 8th grade science Regents results
   - B. Performance in comparison with statewide results for the Asian subgroup on English Language Arts and Mathematics examinations.
   - C. Adequate Yearly Progress for participation in all academic areas for all subgroups.
   - D. The All Students subgroup performance in English Language Arts and Mathematics exceeded the statewide averages.

2. In reviewing the data, the principal, Dr. Finger, identified an area of concern:
   - A. Students with Disabilities performing below the statewide averages in English Language Arts and Mathematics.
   - B. Students in the poverty subgroup performed

48

*below the statewide average on the Grade 8
Science assessment.*

C. *The students identified as General Education
performed below the statewide averages on the
English Language Arts assessment for grades 6,
7 and 8.*

D. *Delta Middle School did not make AYP in
English Language Arts for any subgroup.*

3. *In his analysis of the data regarding his school, Dr.
Finger found the following issue to be worthy of
investigation:*

A. *The high suspension rate.*

B. *A high percent of Students with Disabilities
(SWDs) underperforming on English Language
Arts and Mathematics assessments.*

C. *A large percent of Developing and Ineffective
rated teachers.*

D. *A large percent of English Language Learners
underperforming on all assessments.*

4. *In reviewing the data regarding Adequate Yearly
Progress (AYP), principal Finger expressed concern about
all the following issues, except:*

A. *The Asian subgroup achieved Adequate Yearly
Progress in English Language Arts,
Mathematics and Science.*

B. *The Students with Disabilities subgroup
achieved Adequate Yearly Progress in English
Language Arts and Science but did not for
Mathematics.*

C. *The White subgroup achieved Adequate Yearly
Progress in English Language Arts,
Mathematics and Science.*

D. The Black subgroup achieved Adequate Yearly
   Progress in English Language Arts,
   Mathematics and Science.

<u>Performance Task:</u>
1. What are two primary issues presented in this scenario,
and why do you believe this to be so?

2. What are two important questions you must address
in order to explore this issue? Explain why each is
important to address.

3. How will you go about getting answers to each question?
What challenges might you face in getting answers to your
questions?

4. Describe one possible finding of your inquiry process and
the potential action that finding would imply.

Echo Alternative High School

Courtesy of Chris DeRidder. Shutterstock

Mr. Green, Principal
212 Students
13 Teachers

Echo Alternative High School

Echo Alternative High School is a grade 9-12 school designed to help students who have not been successful attending a typical urban high school for a variety of reasons. The high school is located in an urban area and has an enrollment of 212 students. Students are typically overage and under-credited and have exited from a traditional high school because of academic, social and/or emotional issues. Parent involvement is almost non-existent. Classes are quite different from the typical high school, as students struggle with requirements for graduation. The principal, Mr. Green, was appointed earlier this year; he is respected and liked by teachers and students. Teachers and the principal and assistant principal work collaboratively to consistently use student data and adjust instruction to meet students' needs. The school data committee includes teachers and principal/assistant principal and is managed by a full time data coach who works with colleagues to use formative and summative data to inform instruction. A number of issues have arisen as a result of data-driven instruction.

Discussion

The leadership characteristics and strategies used to facilitate the use of data at the school include:

- Establishing a clear vision for the use of data:
  As an alternative high school, teachers and school leaders regularly work collaboratively to use data to modify and adjust instruction.
- Providing supports that promote a data-driven environment:
  The principal has a full time data coach and an active school data committee that promotes the use of data-driven instruction.

- Making data an ongoing part of the improvement process:
  Since this is an alternative high school with a unique population, students' success in moving towards graduation is marked by effective use of data as exemplified by the Four Year Graduation Rate (Table 7).
- Creating a process or structure to analyze data:
  The principal has facilitated data analysis through a school data committee and more importantly by establishing a full time school data coach.
- Teaching students to examine their own data:
  There is no evidence that students are examining their own data.
- Providing professional development on what the data tells you and how to use it:
  The data coach's responsibility is to provide ongoing professional development by working collaboratively with teachers on examining their data and modifying instruction to maximize students' success.
- Facilitating an organizational culture that supports data use for continuous improvement:
  The principal and assistant principal have facilitated a data-driven culture by creating a school data committee which is led by a teacher (the school's data coach). Data-driven instruction is permeated throughout the teaching/learning environment.
- Providing teacher/data coach leadership:
  The data coach reviews and analyzes data and works with teachers to modify and adjust instruction.

Table 1: Staffing

Principal	1
Assistant Principals	1
Total teachers	13
Teacher turnover rate	17%
Teachers teaching out of license	0
Percent teachers with less than 3 years	8%
Percent teachers with Master's + 30	54%
Percent teachers not highly qualified	0
Ineffective rating (number/%)	0/0
Developing rating (number/%)	4/30%
Effective rating (number/%)	8/62%
Highly Effective rating (number/%)	1/8%

Table 2: Student Demographics

Total Pop.	Black	Hispanic	Asian	White	ELL	SWD	Suspensions	Attend.	Free/Red Lunch
	43%	50%	1%	5%	0	10%	0	72%	79%
212	92	107	2	11	0	21	0		167

Table 3: High School Completers

	Graduates + IEP	Regents Diploma		Adv. Regents Diploma		Non-Completers	
		Number	%	Number	%	Number	%
All Students	95	88	93	0	0	44	21
Gen Education	87	84	97	0	0		
SWD	8	4	50	0	0		

Table 4: Post-Graduation Plans of Completers

	Four Year College		Two Year College		Military		Employment		Unknown	
	#	%	#	%	#	%	#	%	#	%
All Students	7	7	71	75	2	2	1	1	11	12
Gen Education	7	8	63	72	2	2	1	1	11	12
SWD	0	0	8	100	0	0	0	0	0	0

54

Table 5a: Comprehensive English Regents Results

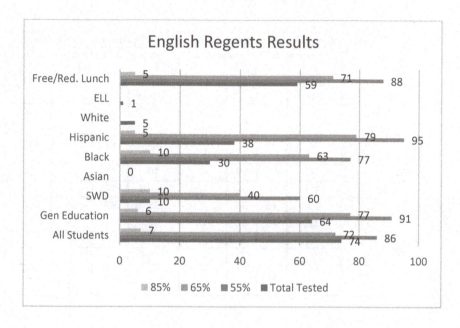

English Regents Results

	85%	65%	55%	Total Tested
Free/Red. Lunch	5	59	71	88
ELL	1			
White	5	5		
Hispanic	5	38	79	95
Black	10	30	63	77
Asian	0			
SWD	10	10	40	60
Gen Education	6	64	77	91
All Students	7	72	74	86

Table 5b: Algebra/ Living Environment Regents Examination Results

	Living Environment				Integrated Algebra			
	(Percent of students scoring at or above)				(Percent of students scoring at or above)			
	Total # Tested	55	65	85	Total # Tested	55	65	85
All Students	37	86	68	3	49	78	47	0
Gen Education	35	--	--	--	45	--	--	--
SWD	2	--	--	--	4	--	--	--
Asian	--	--	--	--	--	--	--	--
Black	19	84	68	0	22	--	--	--
Hispanic	15	--	--	--	24	71	42	0
White	2	--	--	--	3	--	--	--
ELL	--	--	--	--	1	--	--	--
Free/Red. Lunch	29	86	62	0	38	79	47	0

Table 5c: History Regents Examination Results

	Global History and Geography (Percent of students scoring at or above)				US History and Government (Percent of students scoring at or above)			
	Total # Tested	55	65	85	Total # Tested	55	65	85
All Students	74	73	53	3	88	83	60	14
Gen Education	69	74	52	3	78	82	60	14
SWD	5	60	60	0	10	90	90	10
Asian	0	--	--	--	2	--	--	--
Black	36	75	56	3	38	87	58	11
Hispanic	33	73	52	0	40	78	55	5
White	4	--	--	--	7	--	--	--
ELL	3	--	--	--	2	--	--	--
Free/Red. Lunch	56	71	54	2	65	80	60	12

Table 6: Accountability - Adequate Yearly Progress - AYP Participation

	English Language Arts			Mathematics			Overall Accountability
	Made AYP	95% Tested	Safe Harbor	Made AYP	95% Tested	Safe Harbor	Made AYP
All Students	YES	YES	YES	NO	--	NO	YES
Asian	--	--	--	--	--	--	--
Black	YES	YES	YES	NO	YES	NO	YES
Hispanic	NO	YES	NO	NO	YES	NO	YES
White	--	--	--	--	--	--	--
SWD	--	--	--	--	--	--	--
ELL	--	--	--	--	--	--	--
Free/Red. Lunch	NO	--	NO	NO	YES	NO	YES

Table 7: Graduation Rate Accountability – Four Year Rate

	Met Graduation Rate	Graduation Rate	State Standard	Progress Target
All Students	YES	42%	80%	41%
Asian	--	--	--	--
Black	YES	41%	80%	41%
Hispanic	YES	46%	80%	41%
White	--	--	--	--
SWD	--	--	--	--
ELL	--	--	--	--
Free/Red. Lunch	YES	43%	80%	40%

Table 8: Graduation Rate Accountability – Five Year Rate

	Met Graduation Rate	Graduation Rate	State Standard	Progress Target
All Students	NO	58%	80%	68%
Asian	--	--	--	--
Black	YES	81%	80%	67%
Hispanic	NO	57%	80%	70%
White	--	--	--	--
SWD	--	--	--	--
ELL	--	--	--	--
Free/Red. Lunch	NO	55%	80%	67%

Selected Response:

1. In comparing the four year graduation rate with the five year graduation rates, the following statement is incorrect:

    A. All Students met both the four year and five year graduation rates.

B. Black students met both the four year and five year graduation rates.

C. Hispanic students did not meet the four year and five year graduation rates.

D. The Progress Targets for graduation differed for the four year and five year rates.

2. In reviewing Table 6 on Adequate Yearly Progress, which of the following statements is correct:

A. The Black student subgroup made Adequate Yearly Progress for both English Language Arts and Mathematics.

B. The Hispanic student subgroup made Adequate Yearly Progress for both English Language Arts and Mathematics.

C. All Students subgroup did not make Adequate Yearly Progress for both English Language Arts and Mathematics.

D. The Free and Reduced Lunch subgroup did not make Adequate Yearly Progress for both English Language Arts and Mathematics.

3. In analyzing Table 3 High School Completers, the following statement is correct:

A. In the All Students subgroup, ten students received neither a Regents diploma nor an Advanced Regents Diploma.

B. Of the eight graduates in the SWDs subgroup, four received an advanced Regents diploma.

C. Less than 90% of General Education students graduated with a Regents diploma.

D. 21% of All Students did not complete high school.

4. In examining Table 5 Regents Results the following statement is correct:
    A. The largest number of students completed the Living Environment Regents.
    B. SWDs had the lowest percent of students scoring in the 85 and above range.
    C. The performance for the Asian subgroup is mostly unknown due to the insufficient numbers for accountability purposes.
    D. Looking at the Comprehensive English examination, the Hispanic subgroup scored the lowest in the 65% and above category.

Performance Task:

1. Identify one strength of this school, citing evidence to support your response.

2. Identify three areas of need in the instructional program, citing evidence to support each need.

3. Which area of need would be your highest priority? Explain.

4. What are two important questions you must answer to address your highest priority area of need? Explain why each question is important to address. Must relate to Q3.

5. How will you go about getting answers to EACH question?

6. What actions would you take to address the school's priority need? Explain why. Refer to Q3.

7. How would you leverage the identified strength of the school to address the priority need? Refer to Q1.

8. *What possible challenges might your actions create and what are some ways that you could manage these challenges? Refer to Q6.*

Foxtrot Elementary School

Courtesy of Jörg Carstensen. Pearson Education Ltd

Dr. Fourman, Principal
631 Students
33 Teachers

Foxtrot Elementary School

Foxtrot Elementary School is a grade K-5 school located in a blue-collar community within a large metropolitan city. It has 631 students that come from a variety of ethnic backgrounds. There are 33 teachers on staff. The principal, Dr. Fourman, has recently received tenure and is suported by two assistant principals. When the superintendent met with Dr. Fourman at his end of year evaluation he ordered the principal to aggressively address academic deficiencies. Dr. Fourman and his assistant principals decided that engaging teachers in leadership roles within the school would be the vehicle they would employ to address academic deficiencies. Thus a school data team, grade leaders, a professional development committee and a school governance committee were established. Each administrator participated on at least one committee and shared their experiences at weekly cabinet meetings. Furthermore, parents are concerned about their children's education but, because of work, minimally participate in school activities and committees.

Discussion

The leadership characteristics and strategies used to facilitate the use of data at the school include:

- Establishing a clear vision for the use of data:
  Dr. Fourman and his assistant principals recognized that to address the school's academic issues, teachers must become participants in leadership and the use of data. The principal created a school governance committee, grade leader positions, a professional development committee and a school data team.
- Providing supports that promote a data-driven environment:

The school data team and grade leaders provide support for teachers' use of data to inform instruction.

- Making data an ongoing part of the improvement process:
  By engaging teachers in a variety of leadership opportunities and with administrative support, school improvement opportunities are amplified.
- Creating a process or structure to analyze data:
  The school data analyzes achievement data, both formative and summative, and includes grade leaders and school leaders to develop next steps.
- Teaching students to examine their own data:
  There is no evidence to support that students examine their own data.
- Providing professional development on what the data tells you and how to use it:
  The interconnection of the data team, grade leaders and the professional development committee would provide opportunities for data-driven professional development.
- Facilitating an organizational culture that supports data use for continuous improvement:
  By establishing a variety of opportunities to empower teachers, the administrative team is seeking to shift the school's culture to become open to ongoing professional development and more collaborative.
- Providing teacher/data coach leadership:
  Although no formal data coach position has been established, grade leaders are assuming similar responsibilities.

Table 1: Staffing

Principal	1
Assistant Principal	2
Total teachers	33
Teacher turnover rate	17%
Teachers teaching out of license	3%
Percent teachers with less than 3 years	17%
Percent teachers with Master's + 30	37%
Percent teachers not highly qualified	3%
Ineffective rating (number/%)	1/3%
Developing rating (number/%)	3/9%
Effective rating (number/%)	29/88%
Highly Effective rating (number/%)	0/0%

Table 2: Student Demographics

Total Pop.	Black	Hispanic	Asian	White	ELL	SWD	Suspensions	Attend.	Free/Red Lunch
	73%	16%	9%	1%	2%	18%	1%	93%	87%
631	462	103	56	10	11	112	5		548

Table 3: English Language Arts Achievement

	Grade 3: % scoring at level:					Grade 4: % scoring at level:					Grade 5: % scoring at level:				
	1	2	3	4	3+4	1	2	3	4	3+4	1	2	3	4	3+4
Statewide	32	37	28	4	32	31	37	23	10	33	36	35	20	9	29
All Students	44	44	11	1	12	32	44	20	4	24	46	46	8	0	8
Gen Education	38	49	12	1	13	22	48	25	5	30	34	55	11	0	11
SWD	85	8	8	0	8	71	29	0	0	0	80	20	0	0	0
Asian	57	29	14	0	14	--	--	--	--	--	60	20	20	0	20
Black	45	41	14	0	14	33	43	21	3	24	44	50	6	0	6
Hispanic	42	58	0	0	0	36	43	7	14	21	20	55	35	10	0
Poverty	46	42	11	1	12	32	45	20	4	24	46	45	9	0	9

Table 4: Mathematics Achievement

	Grade 3: % scoring at level:					Grade 4: % scoring at level:					Grade 5: % scoring at level:				
	1	2	3	4	3+4	1	2	3	4	3+4	1	2	3	4	3+4
Statewide	27	31	26	16	42	27	31	24	18	42	32	29	24	15	39
All Students	46	36	10	6	16	35	33	26	7	33	45	30	22	3	25
Gen Education	43	39	12	5	17	24	37	29	9	38	40	29	27	4	31
SWD	62	31	0	8	8	75	15	10	0	10	65	35	0	0	0
Asian	43	29	14	14	28	--	--	--	--	--	--	--	--	--	--
Black	48	39	8	6	14	35	35	23	7	30	43	31	22	4	26
Hispanic	33	50	17	0	17	50	14	36	0	36	62	24	14	0	14
Poverty	47	37	11	5	16	33	35	24	8	33	45	28	24	3	27

Table 5: Accountability - Adequate Yearly Progress (AYP)

	English Language Arts			Mathematics		
	Made AYP Perf.	95% Tested	Safe Harbor	Made AYP Perf.	95% Tested	Safe Harbor
All Students	NO	YES	NO	YES	YES	YES
Asian	--	--	--	--	--	--
Black	YES	YES	YES	YES	YES	YES
Hispanic	YES	YES	YES	YES	YES	YES
SWD	NO	YES	NO	NO	YES	NO
Free/Red. Lunch	YES	YES	YES	YES	YES	YES

Selected Response:

1. Using the data provided in Tables 1-5, Dr. Fourman identified all the following as issues of concern at Foxtrot Elementary School, except:

     A. 17% turnover rate for teachers

B 0% teachers identified as highly effective
C. Low performance of SWDs in English Language
   Arts and Mathematics
D. Black and Hispanic subgroups made AYP in
   English Language Arts and Mathematics

2. Using Table 4, which subgroup overall had the lowest
performance in Levels 3+4 in Mathematics?
   A. Asian
   B. Black
   C. SWDs
   D. Hispanic

3. Dr. Fourman looked at the Accountability Table (Table
5) and identified the following issue:
   A. The all Students subgroup met AYP for
      Mathematics but not for English Language Arts.
   B. The Black Students subgroup made AYP for
      English Language Arts but not for Mathematics.
   C. The Hispanic Students subgroup did not make
      AYP for either English Language Arts or
      Mathematics.
   D. The SWDs subgroup made AYP for performance
      because 95% were tested.

4. Comparing the Foxtrot Elementary School's
achievement for All Students in English Language Arts and
Mathematics to statewide averages, Dr. Fourman found:
   A. Foxtrot Elementary School surpassed the
      statewide averages for Level 3+4 in English
      Language Arts, grades 3, 4 and 5.
   B. Foxtrot Elementary school surpassed the
      statewide averages for Level 3+4 in
      Mathematics, grades 3, 4 and 5.

C. The statewide average for Level 3+4 surpassed Foxtrot Elementary School Level 3+4 in English Language Arts in grades 3, 4, and 5.

D. The statewide average for Level 3+4 did not surpass Foxtrot Elementary School Level 3+4 in Mathematics in grades 3, 4, and 5.

Performance Task:

1. Identify one strength of the school, citing evidence to support your response.

2. Identify three areas of need in the instructional program, citing evidence to support each need.

3. Which area of need would be your highest priority? Explain why.

4. What are two important questions you must answer to address your highest priority? Explain why each question is important to address.

5. How will you go about getting answers to each question?

6. What actions would you take to address the school's priority need? Explain why.

7. How would you leverage the identified strength of the school to address the priority need?

8. What possible challenges might your actions create and what are some ways that you could manage these challenges?

Gulf Elementary School

Courtesy of James R. Martin. Shutterstock

339 Students
29 Teachers

Gulf Elementary School

Gulf Elementary School is a K-5 school located in an affluent suburban community. Many of the parents work in the large metropolitan city several miles away. The Parents Association is quite active and participates and/or sponsors a number of school committees and after school or evening activities that supports the positive culture that is identified by this school. The principal is newly appointed; previously she served as an assistant principal in one of the district's middle schools. Upon her selection, she indicated that she wanted to be a transparent and collaborative leader, taking input in her decision-making from all constituencies to create an extremely collaborative culture. There are 29 teachers and 339 students coming from middle class, high socio-economic backgrounds. The children love coming to school, in a stress-free yet highly academic environment. The school has been designated as a Blue Ribbon School by the US Department of Education. Thusly, there is an active school management committee with representatives from all participating groups. Although there is neither a data coach nor assistant principal, it is part of regular practice that teachers use data to inform their instructional decisions. Grade leaders assume great responsibility for instructional leadership and share data-driven decisions with their colleagues. Professional development comes as a result of decisions by the school management committee based upon input from grade leaders, the principal and instructional goals.

Discussion
The leadership characteristics and strategies used to facilitate the use of data at the school include:
- Establishing a clear vision for the use of data:

There is a clear vision for the use of data at the school. Although newly appointed, the principal is supportive of mechanisms established that use data to drive instruction. The principal has stated her vision that she intends to be transparent and collaborative. If those mechanisms were not present, then the school would not be labeled a Blue Ribbon School by the US Department of Education.

- Providing supports that promote a data-driven environment:
  The school management committee, grade leaders and the transparency of the principal drive the data-driven environment.

- Making data an ongoing part of the improvement process:
  Data-driven instruction is supported by the school management committee and grade leaders' use of assessment results to underscore the importance of using data and its relationship to professional development. The transparency of the newly hired principal likewise serves as a support to this collaborative process.

- Creating a process or structure to analyze data:
  The newly hired principal supports grade leaders who serve as instructional coaches with regard to reviewing their colleagues' assessment results to match data with instructional practice.

- Teaching students to examine their own data:
  There is no evidence regarding students examining their own data.

- Providing professional development on what the data tells you and how to use it:
  The school's professional development program is the result of a collaboration of the school management committee, grade leaders and the

principal. Decisions for the type and length of professional development are data-driven.

- Facilitating an organizational culture that supports data use for continuous improvement:
The school has structures in place that facilitate a positive culture because of the participation of all constituencies in school functions, for example, school management committee and active parent organization.
- Providing teacher/data coach leadership: Although there are no data coaches, teacher leadership is encouraged with the use of grade leaders who provide curricular alignment, instructional strategies and assessment analysis to work with their colleagues on each grade.

Table 1: Staffing

Principal	1
Assistant Principal	0
Total teachers	29
Teacher turnover rate	0
Teachers teaching out of license	0
Percent teachers with less than 3 years	0%
Percent teachers with Master's + 30	81%
Percent teachers not highly qualified	0%
Ineffective rating (number/%)	0/0%
Developing rating (number/%)	0/0%
Effective rating (number/%)	9/31%
Highly Effective rating (number/%)	20/69%

Table 2: Student Demographics

Total Pop.	Black	Hispanic	Asian	White	ELL	SWD	Suspensions	Attend.	Free/Red Lunch
	2%	3%	27%	68%	4%	12%	1%	98%	1%
339	5	10	92	231	12	40	4		3

Table 3: English Language Arts Achievement
Three Year Cohort Performance

	2011-12 Grade 3: % scoring at level:					2012-13 Grade 4: % scoring at level:					2013-2014 Grade 5: % scoring at level:				
	1	2	3	4	3+4	1	2	3	4	3+4	1	2	3	4	3+4
Statewide	37	31	28	4	32	31	37	23	10	33	36	35	20	9	29
All Students	12	28	47	13	60	9	38	33	21	53	5	37	42	15	57
Gen Education	8	25	51	16	67	6	36	36	22	58	0	33	49	18	67
SWD	33	44	22	0	22	25	50	13	13	26	30	60	10	0	10
Asian	--	--	--	--	--	--	--	--	--	--	--	--	--	--	--
Black	--	--	--	--	--	--	--	--	--	--	--	--	--	--	--
Hispanic	--	--	--	--	--	--	--	--	--	--	--	--	--	--	--
Poverty	--	--	--	--	--	--	--	--	--	--	--	--	--	--	--

*Cohort analyses assumes performance of the same students across the three years.

Table 4: Mathematics Achievement
Three Year Cohort Performance

	2011-2012 Grade 3: % scoring at level:					2012-2013 Grade 4: % scoring at level:					2013-2014 Grade 5: % scoring at level:				
	1	2	3	4	3+4	1	2	3	4	3+4	1	2	3	4	3+4
Statewide	27	31	26	16	42	27	31	24	18	42	32	29	24	15	39
All Students	8	18	35	38	73	4	22	29	45	74	5	17	50	28	78
Gen Education	4	18	35	43	78	0	18	33	49	82	2	15	54	29	83
SWD	33	22	33	11	44	33	50	0	17	17	33	33	17	17	34
Asian	--	--	--	--	--	--	--	--	--	--	0	7	53	40	93
Black	--	--	--	--	--	--	--	--	--	--	--	--	--	--	--
Hispanic	--	--	--	--	--	--	--	--	--	--	--	--	--	--	--
Poverty	--	--	--	--	--	--	--	--	--	--	--	--	--	--	--

*Cohort analyses assumes performance of the same students across the three years.

Table 5: Accountability - Adequate Yearly Progress (AYP)

	English Language Arts			Mathematics		
	Made AYP	95% Tested	Safe Harbor	Made AYP	95% Tested	Safe Harbor
All Students	YES	YES	YES	YES	YES	YES
Asian	YES	YES	YES	YES	YES	YES
Black	--	--	--	--	--	--
Hispanic	--	--	--	--	--	--
SWD	--	--	--	--	--	--
Free/Red. Lunch	--	--	--	--	--	--

Selected Response:

1. *Looking at the data for Gulf Elementary School, the most pressing issue is:*
   - A. *The number of teachers identified as developing.*
   - B. *The All Students subgroup performance in Mathematics.*
   - C. *The overall achievement of SWDs.*
   - D. *The Adequate Yearly Progress for All Students.*

2. *One goal the newly appointed principal of this school might consider:*
   - A. *Increasing parent involvement.*
   - B. *Increasing the performance for All Students.*
   - C. *Increasing professional development opportunities for not highly qualified teachers.*
   - D. *The high teacher turnover rate.*

3. *In reviewing the information presented in Table 3, which of the following statements is NOT true*

A. The most progress for this cohort was demonstrated by the All Students subgroup in 2012-2013.
B. The performance of the General Education group was inconsistent for this cohort of students.
C. The performance of the All Students subgroup exceeded that of the state for the three identified years.
D. Students identified as SWDs were not tested over this three-year period of time.

4. The data in Table 4 indicates all of the following reasons except:
   A. The SWDs subgroup is performing significantly below that of their peers.
   B. There aren't enough students in the Asian, Black, Hispanic and Poverty subgroups to measure their performance.
   C. The statewide averages are at least 30 percentage points below that of the All Students subgroup for all grade levels provided.
   D. The All Students subgroup outperformed all other categories.

Performance Task:

1. What are two primary issues presented in this scenario, and why do you believe this to be so?

2. What are two important questions you must address in order to explore this issue? Explain why each is important to address.

74

3. How will you go about getting answers to each question? What challenges might you face in getting answers to your questions?

4. Describe one possible finding of your inquiry process and the potential action that finding would imply.

Hotel Middle School

Courtesy of Konstantin L. Shutterstock

Mr. Susino, Principal
813 Students
104 Teachers

Hotel Middle School

Hotel Middle School is located 15 miles north of the state capital in an affluent suburban/rural community. The school is situated on a sprawling campus and has 813 students in grades six, seven and eight. The principal, Mr. Susino, has been the leader of the school for the past five years. He is supported by an assistant principal having twelve years of experience. There is extensive parent partnership in all aspects of school life. Parents volunteer throughout the school and participate in school governance and data committees. Many parents work in the nearby technology park and are experts in a variety of technologies. Therefore, parents have spearheaded use of technology in the school. As such, the principal writes a regular blog and every teacher has his/her own web page which includes students' assignments and projects, providing parents and their children opportunities to examine their school work and grades. Department chairpersons and lead teachers have taken leadership in mentoring their colleagues to use technology and how to effectively use data to improve teaching and learning. Although a highly successful middle school, it is not without problems or challenges.

Discussion

The leadership characteristics and strategies used to facilitate the use of data at the school include:

- Establishing a clear vision for the use of data:
  The school principal has embraced that transparency is important to the school community. Teachers share their students' grades and assignments via the internet. The school has a data committee including the principal or assistant principal, teachers and parents.

- Providing supports that promote a data-driven environment:
  The school promotes a data-driven environment via the use of technology by all constituents. Teacher web pages, principal communiques and parents having access to their students' grades and assignments facilitates a data-driven environment.
- Making data an ongoing part of the improvement process:
  The school data committee along with department chairpersons and lead teachers are supportive of using technology to share data.
- Creating a process or structure to analyze data:
  With department chairpersons and lead teachers modeling use of data and structuring parents' access to students' information on web pages, a structure for data analysis is in place. Additionally, department chairpersons and lead teachers share data findings with their colleagues.
- Teaching students to examine their own data: Teacher web pages give students' and their parents opportunities to examine their own data to help them determine next steps.
- Providing professional development on what the data tells you and how to use it:
  Department chairpersons and lead teachers provide training for using data. This serves as a platform for school wide professional development. Additionally, parent expertise lends a helping hand to further cement the relationship between school, the parent community and ongoing professional development.
- Facilitating an organizational culture that supports data use for continuous improvement:
  The school exhibits a positive culture in which school leaders, teachers and parents are partners

in their children's education. Parent volunteerism, parent technology expertise and parent participation in all activities are indicative of their commitment to their children's education. School leaders and teachers support and enrich the technology driven environment as well thereby reinforcing a collaborative culture.

- Providing teacher/data coach leadership: Although there are no formal data coaches, there are department chairpersons and teacher leaders to help colleagues with understanding their students' data and using web pages effectively.

Table 1: Staffing

Principal	1
Assistant Principals	1
Total teachers	104
Teacher turnover rate	16%
Teachers teaching out of license	0
Percent teachers with less than 3 years	6%
Percent teachers with Master's + 30	10%
Percent teachers not highly qualified	0%
Ineffective rating (number/%)	0
Developing rating (number/%)	0
Effective rating (number/%)	12/24%
Highly Effective rating (number/%)	39/76%

Table 2: Student Demographics

Total Pop.	Black	Hispanic	Asian	White	ELL	SWD	Suspensions	Attend.	Free/Red Lunch
	5%	4%	9%	82%	--	11%	1%	96%	8%
813	39	30	76	668	--	93	5		65

Table 3: English Language Arts Achievement

	Grade 6: % scoring at level:					Grade 7: % scoring at level:					Grade 8: % scoring at level:				
	1	2	3	4	3+4	1	2	3	4	3+4	1	2	3	4	3+4
Statewide	29	42	16	14	30	32	37	23	8	31	30	37	23	10	33
All Students	9	32	25	34	59	12	29	41	18	59	8	27	41	24	65
Gen Education	5	32	26	37	63	7	30	44	20	64	3	26	44	26	70
SWD	63	26	5	5	10	74	26	0	0	0	46	35	15	4	19
Asian	4	19	38	38	76	8	16	24	52	76	9	9	23	59	82
Black	17	50	0	33	33	0	44	56	0	56	--	--	--	--	--
Hispanic	25	50	13	13	26	14	57	29	0	29	--	--	--	--	--
White	8	31	25	36	61	12	30	42	16	58	8	30	39	23	62
Poverty	20	37	17	27	43	25	38	38	0	38	20	27	27	27	54

Table 4: Mathematics Achievement

	Grade 6: % scoring at level:					Grade 7: % scoring at level:					Grade 8: % scoring at level:				
	1	2	3	4	3+4	1	2	3	4	3+4	1	2	3	4	3+4
Statewide	29	41	18	12	30	38	34	20	7	27	31	41	20	7	27
All Students	7	30	26	37	63	9	36	37	18	56	9	37	43	11	54
Gen Education	3	29	28	39	67	5	35	40	20	60	4	35	48	12	60
SWD	53	37	5	5	10	56	44	0	0	0	46	50	4	0	4
Asian	0	7	15	78	93	0	25	30	45	75	0	33	50	17	67
Black	0	67	17	17	34	33	22	33	11	44	--	--	--	--	--
Hispanic	31	31	13	25	38	29	29	29	14	43	14	57	29	0	29
White	6	31	30	34	64	3	37	39	16	55	10	36	43	11	54
Poverty	10	31	38	21	59	29	42	25	4	29	19	59	22	0	22

Table 5: Science-Grade 8 vs. Regents Grade 8

| | Science Grade 8 | | | | | Regents Grade 8 (Living Environment) | | | | |
| | % scoring level: | | | | | % scoring level: | | | | |
	1	2	3	4	3+4	1	2	3	4	3+4
Statewide	6	21	43	30	73					
All Students	1	8	41	50	91	0	0	0	100	100
Gen Education	0	4	38	57	95					
SWD	7	29	57	7	64					
Asian	0	8	15	77	92					
Black	--	--	--	--	--					
Hispanic	0	13	50	38	88					
White	1	7	42	49	91					
Poverty	0	23	53	23	76					

Table 6: Mathematics Regents Examination Results

| | Integrated Algebra (Percent of students scoring at or above) | | | | Geometry (Percent of students scoring at or above) | | | |
	Total Tested	55	65	85	Total Tested	55	65	85
All Students	49	100	100	71	13	100	100	92
Gen Education	49	100	100	71	13	100	100	92
SWD	--	--	--	--	--	--	--	--
Asian	12	--	--	--	3	--	--	--
Black	1	--	--	--	0	0	0	0
Hispanic	--	--	--	--	--	--	--	--
White	36	100	100	69	10	--	--	--
ELL	--	--	--	--		--	-	--
Free/Red. Lunch	--	--	--	--		--	-	--

Table 7: Earth Science Regents Examination Results

	Earth Science (Percent of students scoring at or above)			
	Total # Tested	55	65	85
All Students	46	100	100	100
Gen Education	46	100	100	100
SWD	--	--	--	--
Asian	9	--	--	--
Black	1	--	--	--
Hispanic	--	--	--	--
White	36	100	100	100
ELL	--	--	--	--
Free/Red. Lunch	--	--	--	--

Table 8: Accountability - Adequate Yearly Progress (AYP)

	English Language Arts			Mathematics			Science		
	Made AYP	95% Tested	Safe Harbor	Made AYP	95% Tested	Safe Harbor	Made AYP	95% Tested	Safe Harbor
All Students	YES	YES	YES	YES	YES	YES	YES	YES	YES
Asian	YES	YES	YES	YES	YES	--	--	--	--
Black	--	--	--	--	--	--	--	--	--
Hispanic	--	--	--	--	--	--	--	--	--
White	YES	YES	YES	YES	YES	YES	YES	YES	YES
SWD	YES	YES	YES	YES	YES	YES	YES	--	YES
ELL	--	--	--	--	--	--	--	--	--
Free/Red Lunch	YES	YES	YES	YES	YES	YES	YES	--	YES

Selected Response:

1. The principal, Mr. Susino, examined state achievement test results in English Language Arts and Mathematics. Which one of the following conclusions is correct?

A. In the Hotel Middle School the All Students subgroup consistently performed above the statewide averages for Level 3+4 in English Language Arts and Mathematics.

B. In the Hotel Middle School SWDs consistently performed above the statewide averages for Level 3+4 in Reading and Mathematics.

C. In the Hotel Middle School, the Hispanic subgroup consistently performed above the statewide averages for Level 3+4 in English Language Arts and Mathematics.

D. In the Hotel Middle School the Poverty subgroup consistently performed above the statewide averages for Level 3+4 in English Language Arts and Mathematics.

2. In evaluating the results from the Mathematics and Science Regents examinations, which of the following statement is correct:

A. A large number of students participated in the Mathematics Regents examinations.

B. The Asian Subgroup performed at the same level as General Education students.

C. Regents examinations were administered to a small number of students and excluded representation from a number of subgroups.

D. More students participated in the Geometry Regents than the Algebra Regents examination.

3. Looking at Tables 1-8, Mr. Susino determined:

A. With 1% of the population suspended, there is a great need for stricter disciplinary controls.

B. There is a need for a program for English Language Learners.

C. Student attendance needs his full attention.

D. Although there is a small population of minority subgroups, attention needs to be paid to their academic achievement.

4. Looking at Table 1, which statement is incorrect?

A. With 51 teachers on staff, 8 teachers have left the school.

B. With 51 teachers on staff, approximately 5 teachers have a master's degree+30 credits.

C. With 51 teachers on staff, all teachers were rated either effective or highly effective/

D. With 51 teachers on staff, approximately 6 teachers have less than 3 years' experience.

Performance Task:

1. Give one strength of Hotel Middle School. What evidence would you use to support this determination? What strategy might you use to enhance this strength?

2. List three areas of need for Hotel Middle School. What evidence would you use to support this determination?

3. Which area of need would be your highest priority? Explain why.

4. What are two important questions you must answer to address your highest priority? Explain why each question is important to address.

5. How would you go about getting answers to each question?

6. What actions would you take to address the school's priority need? Explain why.

7. How would you leverage the identified strength of the school to address the priority need?

8. What possible challenges might your actions create and what are some ways that you could manage these challenges?

India Expeditionary Secondary School

Courtesy of Jules Selmes. Pearson Education Ltd

Mr. Pope, Principal
607 Students
43 Teachers

India Expeditionary Learning Secondary School

India Expeditionary Learning Secondary School is a grade 6-12 school designed around a theme of expeditionary learning. Students engage in reality-based, hands-on learning activities called expeditions. Teachers work collaboratively to construct learning expeditions that integrate multi-disciplinary experiences across curricula and that use formative and summative assessment to inform instruction. The school is located in a large city and accepts students as a result of a selection process. The school was opened a few years ago and contains grades 6-11 with 607 students, adding a 12th grade graduating class this year. The principal, Mr. Pope, founded the school with a group of similar minded teachers. Teachers regularly participate in the school governance committee and the professional development planning committee. Several teachers and department chairpersons have stepped forward to become teacher leaders in the school's ongoing development. Students' self-assessment is part of every learning expedition. Parent participation is better than expected for an urban school since students went through a selection process for admission, some parents are eager to become involved. Professional development is ongoing; teachers are provided ample time to develop new expeditionary learning experiences that are shared amongst their colleagues.

Discussion

The leadership characteristics and strategies used to facilitate the use of data at the school include:
- Establishing a clear vision for the use of data:
  The school was established as a collaborative effort of teachers and its founding principal, Mr. Pope. Through learning expeditions, data is transparently used to inform and modify instruction.

- Providing supports that promote a data-driven environment:
  Teachers are provided ample time to develop data-driven expeditionary learning experiences. The principal is supportive of teachers because they co-founded this secondary school and share the same philosophy for learning.
- Making data an ongoing part of the improvement process:
  Formative and summative data is consistently used to provide input into the instructional program reviewing and modifying expeditionary learning experiences.
- Creating a process or structure to analyze data:
  Assessment is built into expeditionary learning experiences. Students' self-assessment and feedback provide opportunities to use formative data to modify instruction. Working collaboratively, the school's data committee and lead teachers/department chairpersons provide analysis of data for inform practice.
- Providing professional development on what the data tells you and how to use it:
  Professional development is ongoing in developing and refining expeditionary learning experiences. Professional development reflects data analysis so that professional development is constantly focused on improving learning expeditions.
- Facilitating an organizational culture that supports data use for continuous improvement:
  There is a highly collegial culture at this school, especially since teachers founded the school along with the principal. Since such an environment flourishes, assessment is regularly used to drive instruction to move the school towards continuous improvement.

- Providing teacher/data coach leadership: Department chairpersons and lead teachers in each subject area facilitate development of new learning expeditions, working collaboratively with their colleagues in each department.

Table 1: Staffing

Principal	1
Assistant Principals	1
Total teachers	46
Teacher turnover rate	17%
Teachers teaching out of license	24%
Percent teachers with less than 3 years	37%
Percent teachers with Master's + 30	11%
Percent teachers not highly qualified	25%
Ineffective rating (number/%)	1/2%
Developing rating (number/%)	4/9%
Effective rating (number/%)	35/76%
Highly Effective rating (number/%)	6/13%

Table 2: Student Demographics

Total Pop.	Black	Hispanic	Asian	White	ELL	SWD	Suspensions	Attend.	Free/Red Lunch
	130	230	108	139	11	129	6	96%	367
607	22%	38%	18%	23%	2%	21%	1%		61%

Table 3: English Language Arts Achievement

	Grade 6: % scoring at level:					Grade 7: % scoring at level:					Grade 8: % scoring at level:				
	1	2	3	4	3+4	1	2	3	4	3+4	1	2	3	4	3+4
Statewide	29	42	16	14	30	32	37	23	8	31	30	37	23	10	33
All Students	20	43	17	20	37	28	44	25	3	28	24	43	27	6	33
Gen Education	9	46	21	24	45	22	45	30	4	34	16	42	34	8	42
SWD	64	32	0	4	4	61	39	0	0	0	52	44	4	0	4
Asian	5	35	35	25	60	10	52	34	3	37	21	42	25	13	38
Black	36	32	12	20	32	35	45	20	0	20	30	48	22	0	22
Hispanic	27	53	13	7	20	35	45	20	0	20	28	52	21	0	21
White	4	44	16	36	52	--	--	--	--	--	19	30	37	15	52
Poverty	27	47	14	12	26	31	47	20	2	22	28	52	19	2	21

Table 4: Mathematics Achievement

	Grade 6: % scoring at level:					Grade 7: % scoring at level:					Grade 8: % scoring at level:				
	1	2	3	4	3+4	1	2	3	4	3+4	1	2	3	4	3+4
Statewide	29	41	18	12	30	38	34	20	7	27	31	41	20	7	27
All Students	23	26	23	27	50	25	38	30	5	35	45	52	3	0	3
Gen Education	11	26	29	34	63	19	41	34	6	40	38	60	6	0	6
SWD	72	28	0	0	0	65	24	12	0	12	56	40	4	0	4
Asian	5	20	45	30	75	17	28	45	10	55	29	71	0	0	0
Black	36	28	12	24	36	47	47	5	0	5	61	39	0	0	0
Hispanic	33	29	20	18	38	26	45	25	4	29	50	45	5	0	5
White	12	24	20	44	64	--	--	--	--	--	--	--	--	--	--
Poverty	31	29	23	17	40	29	41	28	1	29	50	50	0	0	0

Table 5: Science-Grade 8 Achievement

	% scoring level:				
	1	**2**	**3**	**4**	**3+4**
Statewide	6	21	43	30	73
All Students	16	24	49	12	61
Gen Education	28	40	32	0	32
SWD	28	40	32	0	32
Asian	21	17	38	25	63
Black	17	48	35	0	35
Hispanic	23	23	50	3	53
White	4	11	63	22	85
Poverty	25	28	42	6	48

Table 6a: Mathematics Regents Examination Results

	Integrated Algebra				Algebra 1 Common Core					
	(Percent of students scoring at or above)									
	Total Tested	*55*	*65*	*85*	*Total Tested*	*Level 1= 0-54*	*Level 2= 55-64*	*Level 3= 65-73*	*Level 4= 74-84*	*Level 5= 85-100*
All Students	157	95	83	17	105	5	12	66	15	2
Gen Education	124	96	87	19	84	0	10	71	17	2
SWD	33	91	70	9	21	24	24	43	10	0
Asian	20	100	95	40	14	0	7	43	43	7
Black	24	96	75	8	13	--	--	--	--	--
Hispanic	60	92	82	10	40	3	13	70	15	0
White	48	96	83	21	35	9	14	63	11	3
ELL	5	80	80	0	4	--	--	--	--	--
Free/Red. Lunch	87	91	77	13	58	3	16	66	14	2

Table 6b: Mathematics Regents Examination Results

| | Geometry | | | | Algebra 2/Trigonometry | | | |
	Total Tested	(Percent of students scoring at or above)			Total Tested	(Percent of students scoring at or above)		
	Total Tested	55	65	85	Total Tested	55	65	85
All Students	122	79	61	11	25	76	28	4
Gen Education	101	82	62	14	25	76	28	4
SWD	21	62	52	0	0	0	0	0
Asian	15	80	53	27	7	86	43	0
Black	16	63	19	0	3	--	--	--
Hispanic	52	75	58	6	6	--	--	--
White	34	94	88	18	9	78	11	0
ELL	1	--	--	--	0	0	0	0
Free/Red. Lunch	66	73	48	8	14	71	29	0

Table 7a: Living Environment and Earth Science Regents Examination Results

| | Living Environment | | | | Earth Science | | | |
	Total Tested	(Percent of students scoring at or above)			Total Tested	(Percent of students scoring at or above)		
	Total Tested	55	65	85	Total Tested	55	65	85
All Students	116	98	87	23	73	73	49	15
Gen Education	90	99	90	28	54	76	50	19
SWD	26	96	77	8	19	63	47	5
Asian	10	--	--	--	13	85	62	47
Black	13	100	85	15	11	--	--	--
Hispanic	51	96	82	16	27	67	33	0
White	39	100	92	33	19	84	79	26
ELL	4	--	--	--	1	--	--	--
Free/Red. Lunch	63	97	83	14	43	67	37	7

Table 7b: Chemistry Regents Examination Results

	Chemistry			
		(Percent of students scoring at or above)		
	Total Tested	*55*	*65*	*85*
All Students	41	76	29	0
Gen Education	40	--	--	--
SWD	1	--	--	--
Asian	12	83	42	0
Black	5	--	--	--
Hispanic	13	92	15	0
White	9	89	56	0
ELL	0	0	0	0
Free/Red. Lunch	23	83	30	0

Table 8: History Regents Examination Results

	US History			
		(Percent of students scoring at or above)		
	Total Tested	*55*	*65*	*85*
All Students	22	59	45	0
Gen Education	15	73	53	0
SWD	7	29	29	0
Asian	3	--	--	--
Black	5	--	--	--
Hispanic	13	69	54	0
White	1	--	--	--
ELL	1	--	--	--
Free/Red. Lunch	15	67	53	0

Table 9: Accountability - Adequate Yearly Progress (AYP)

	English Language Arts			Mathematics			Science		
	Made AYP	95% Tested	Safe Harbor	Made AYP	95% Tested	Safe Harbor	Made AYP	95% Tested	Safe Harbor
All Students	YES	YES	YES	YES	YES	YES	NO	YES	NO
Asian	YES	YES	YES	YES	YES	YES	--	--	--
Black	YES	YES	YES	YES	YES	YES	--	--	--
Hispanic	YES	YES	YES	YES	YES	YES	--	--	--
White	YES	YES	YES	YES	YES	YES	--	--	--
SWD	YES	YES	YES	YES	YES	YES	--	--	--
ELL	--	--	--	--	--	--	--	--	--
Free/Red. Lunch	YES	YES	YES	YES	YES	YES	NO	YES	NO

Selected Response:

1. In reviewing the staffing of India Expeditionary Learning Secondary School, it is clear that:
   A. Hardly any teachers are teaching out of license.
   B. There is a large number of highly effective teachers.
   C. All teachers are appropriately licensed.
   D. 37% of the teachers have 3 years or less experience.

2. In evaluating student achievement in English Language Arts and Mathematics in grades 6, 7 and 8, the following generalization holds true:
   A. Levels 3+4 performance for SWDs in English Language Arts and Mathematics is approaching the statewide averages.
   B. The General Education subgroup consistently outperformed the SWDs subgroup on the grades.
   6-8 English Language Arts and Mathematics assessments.

94

C. Levels 3+4 performance for the All Student subgroup in English Language Arts in Grades 6, 7 and 8 is above the statewide averages.
D. Levels 3+4 performance for the All Student subgroup in Mathematics in Grades 6, 7 and 8 is above the statewide averages.

3. In examining the Adequate Yearly Progress (AYP) (Table 9), the following conclusion can be drawn:
    A. The school did not make AYP for English Language Arts
    B. The school did not make AYP for Mathematics.
    C. The school did not make AYP for Science.
    D. The school did not make AYP for the Free/Reduced lunch subgroup for English Language Arts and Mathematics.

4. In reviewing Regents performance in Mathematics, Science and History (Tables 6, 7 & 8), the following conclusion is accurate:
    A. The school evidenced high percentages of achievement at a score of 85% or higher for all subgroups.
    B. The SWDs subgroup evidenced high Percentages of achievement at a score of 85% or higher.
    C. The Black and Hispanic subgroups evidenced high percentages of achievement at a score of 85% or higher.
    D. The school evidenced low performance in the 85% or higher range for most subgroups on all Regents examinations.

Performance Task:

1. What are two primary issues presented in this scenario, and why do you believe this to be so?

2. What are two important questions you must address in order to explore this issue? Explain why each is important to address.

3. How will you go about getting answers to each question? What challenges might you face in getting answers to your questions?

4. Describe one possible finding of your inquiry process and the potential action that finding would imply.

Juliet Middle School

Courtesy of Cynthia Farmer. Shutterstock

586 Students
45 Teachers

Juliet Middle School

Juliet Middle School is located within a large metropolitan city. The school has 586 students in grades six, seven and eight from a mostly economically disadvantaged community. Juliet Middle School has been identified by the State Education Department as *persistently struggling*. You are the newly assigned principal and are supported by three assistant principals. There are 45 teachers on staff, some of whom are not highly qualified. Some teachers teach a number of subjects out of license.

Discussion
The leadership characteristics and strategies used to facilitate the use of data at the school include:
- Establishing a clear vision for the use of data: Juliet Middle School has been designated as *persistently struggling*. There are a number of issues that makes the school dysfunctional including a lack of vision for increasing student achievement. Because you are the newly assigned principal, you must prioritize work to address building your school's vision by engaging stakeholders.
- Providing supports that promote a data-driven environment:
  Currently there are no supports in place to train teachers to implement successful teaching strategies as a result of using data effectively. The only support are the three assistant principals.
- Making data an ongoing part of the improvement process:
  If data was an ongoing part of the school improvement process, then the school would not be persistently struggling. Data has not been used by teachers and school leaders to inform and modify instructional practice.

- Creating a process or structure to analyze data: The new principal and his assistant principals are developing structures to address data-driven instruction. However these structures are currently lacking teacher involvement.
- Teaching students to examine their own data: There are no structures in place that involve students' examining their own data.
- Providing professional development on what the data tells you and how to use it:
  Professional development is needed so that teachers recognize the efficacy of using their own data to inform practice. How to structure such an undertaking must be the collaborative effort of school leaders and teachers which at this point is non-existent.
- Facilitating an organizational culture that supports data use for continuous improvement:
  There is a need to develop a data-driven culture around teaching and learning strategies that involves teachers in developing differentiated instructional practice. The current culture provides no opportunities for teachers' examination of their students' achievement.
- Providing teacher/data coach leadership:
  Table 1 along with the description of Juliet Middle School reinforces that there are no teacher leaders or data coaches that might instruct their colleagues in the use of data to drive instruction. To develop pathways for improvement, it is critical for this middle school to engage teachers at looking at their own data.

Table 1: Staffing

Principal	1
Assistant Principals	3
Total teachers	45
Teacher turnover rate	42%
Teachers teaching out of license	49%
Percent teachers with less than 3 years	36%
Percent teachers with Master's + 30	13%
Percent teachers not highly qualified	40%
Ineffective rating (number/%)	1/2%
Developing rating (number/%)	7/15%
Effective rating (number/%)	37/82%
Highly Effective rating (number/%)	0/0%

Table 2: Student Demographics

Black	Hispanic	Asian	White	LEP	Total	SWD	Suspensions	Attendance	Free/ Red. Lunch
162	399	9	7	195	586	130	38		527
28%	68%	2%	1%	34%		23%	6%	88%	91%

Table 3a: Grade 6 English Language Arts Achievement

	2014 - % scoring at level:					2013 - % scoring at level:				
	1	2	3	4	3+4	1	2	3	4	3+4
Statewide	29	42	16	14	30	32	37	22	9	31
All Students	66	29	4	0	4	67	28	4	1	5
Gen Education	62	33	5	0	5	60	33	5	1	6
SWD	90	10	0	0	0	94	6	0	0	0
Asian	--	--	--	--	--	--	--	--	--	--
Black	--	--	--	--	--	--	--	--	--	--
Hispanic	69	29	2	0	2	66	28	4	1	5
Poverty	68	29	3	0	3	--	--	--	--	--
ELL	89	11	0	0	0	90	10	0	0	0
Non Poverty	50	33	17	0	17	--	--	--	--	--

Table 3b: Grade 7 English Language Arts Achievement

	2014 - % scoring at level:					2013 - % scoring at level:				
	1	2	3	4	3+4	1	2	3	4	3+4
Statewide	32	37	23	8	31	8	39	49	4	51
All Students	70	24	5	1	6	64	29	8	0	8
Gen Education	64	29	6	1	7	60	30	9	0	9
SWD	92	8	0	0	0	79	21	0	0	0
Asian	--	--	--	--	--	--	--	--	--	--
Black	--	--	--	--	--	64	26	9	0	9
Hispanic	73	23	3	2	5	66	27	7	0	7
Poverty	71	23	5	1	6	64	28	8	0	8
ELL	92	8	0	0	0	93	7	0	0	0
Non Poverty	64	36	0	0	0	67	33	0	0	0

Table 3c: Grade 8 English Language Arts Achievement

	2014 - % scoring at level:					2013 - % scoring at level:				
	1	2	3	4	3+4	1	2	3	4	3+4
Statewide	30	37	23	10	33	7	42	48	2	50
All Students	56	36	8	1	9	69	26	4	0	4
Gen Education	52	38	8	1	9	68	27	5	0	5
SWD	69	31	0	0	0	78	22	0	0	0
Asian	--	--	--	--	--	--	--	--	--	--
Black	49	41	8	2	10	61	35	4	0	4
Hispanic	60	32	8	0	8	72	24	4	0	4
Poverty	56	37	7	1	8	69	27	5	0	5
ELL	88	10	2	0	2	87	13	0	0	0
Non Poverty	56	31	13	0	13	80	20	0	0	0

Table 4a: Grade 6 Mathematics Achievement

	2014 - % scoring at level:					2013 - % scoring at level:				
	1	2	3	4	3+4	1	2	3	4	3+4
Statewide	31	33	22	14	36	33	36	21	10	31
All Students	78	21	1	0	1	75	23	2	0	2
Gen Education	75	24	1	0	1	71	26	3	0	3
SWD	95	5	0	0	0	89	11	0	0	0
Asian	--	--	--	--	--	--	--	--	--	--
Black	--	--	--	--	--	--	--	--	--	--
Hispanic	78	22	0	0	0	76	21	3	0	3
Poverty	80	20	1	0	1	--	--	--	--	--
ELL	93	7	0	0	0	63	34	3	0	3
Non Poverty	62	38	0	0	0	--	--	--	--	--

Table 4b: Grade 7 Mathematics Achievement

	2014 % scoring at level:					2013 % scoring at level:				
	1	2	3	4	3+4	1	2	3	4	3+4
Statewide	30	37	23	10	33	7	42	48	2	50
All Students	85	14	1	0	1	78	21	2	0	2
Gen Education	82	16	1	0	1	76	23	2	0	2
SWD	37	95	5	0	0	86	11	3	0	3
Asian	--	--	--	--	--	--	--	--	--	--
Black	--	--	--	--	--	87	11	2	0	2
Hispanic	89	10	2	0	2	75	23	2	0	2
Poverty	85	14	1	0	1	77	21	2	0	2
ELL	97	3	0	0	0	91	7	2	0	2
Non Poverty	92	8	0	0	0	100	0	0	0	0

Table 4c: Grade 8 Mathematics Achievement

	2014 - % scoring at level:					2013 - % scoring at level:				
	1	2	3	4	3+4	1	2	3	4	3+4
Statewide	31	41	20	7	27	7	31	42	20	62
All students	68	30	1	0	1	73	25	2	0	2
Gen Education	64	33	3	0	3	72	26	2	0	2
SWD	85	15	0	0	0	81	19	0	0	0
Asian	--	--	--	--	--	--	--	--	--	--
Black	67	31	2	0	2	79	21	0	0	0
Hispanic	69	29	2	0	2	72	26	2	0	2
Poverty	67	31	2	0	2	73	25	2	0	2
ELL	87	12	2	0	2	90	10	0	0	0
Non Poverty	81	19	0	0	0	78	22	0	0	0

Table 5: Science Achievement-Grade 8

	Science Grade 8				
	% scoring level:				
	1	2	3	4	3+4
Statewide	9	23	40	28	68
All Students	38	44	18	1	18
Gen Education	31	48	20	1	21
SWD	67	23	10	0	10
Asian	--	--	--	--	--
Black	39	41	20	0	20
Hispanic	39	43	17	1	18
White	--	--	--	--	--
ELL	66	27	7	0	7
Poverty	39	42	19	1	20

Table 6: Middle Level English Language Arts, Mathematics and Science Results for Accountability Adequate Yearly Progress (AYP)

	English Language Arts		Mathematics		Science	
	Made AYP	Tested 95%	Made AYP	Tested 95%	Made AYP	Tested 80%
All Students	X	✓	X	✓	X	✓
SWD	X	✓	X	✓	--	
Asian	--	--	--	--	--	
Black	X	✓	X	✓	X	✓
Hispanic	X	✓	X	✓	X	✓
White	--	--	--	--	--	
Poverty	X	✓	X	✓	X	✓
ELL	X	✓	X	✓	X	✓

X=subgroup did not make AYP

Selected Response:

1. All of the following are problems for this persistently struggling middle school, except:

    A. Declining achievement in English Language Arts.

    B. Declining achievement in Mathematics.

    C. Low percent of students having limited English Proficiency.

    D. Not making Adequate Yearly Progress for all subgroups.

2. In looking at Table 6, Accountability Results, which of the groups achieved Adequate Yearly Progress in English Language Arts:

    A. Students with Disabilities

    B. Hispanic

    C. None

    D. All Students

3. In examining staffing (Table 1) at Juliet Middle School, which of the following statements is correct?
   A. There is a low turnover rate.
   B. There is a large number of highly experienced teachers.
   C. Only one teacher was rated ineffective.
   D. 40% of the teachers on staff are considered qualified.

4. The newly assigned principal and assistant principals reviewed the student information as reflected in the Tables above and found the following statement to be true:
   A. English Language Arts and Mathematics achievement declined over two years for the most part.
   B. The low number of limited English proficient students did not affect achievement scores.
   C. All Students subgroup approached the statewide achievement rate in Science.
   D. The school has consistently made Adequate Yearly Progress for all subgroups in English Language Arts, Mathematics and Science

Performance Task:

1. Give one strength of Juliet Middle School. What evidence would you use to support this determination? What strategy might you use to enhance this strength?

2. List three areas of need for Juliet Middle School. What evidence would you use to support this determination?

3. Which area of need would be your highest priority? Explain why.

105

4. *What are two important questions you must answer to address your highest priority? Explain why each question is important to address.*

5. *How would you go about getting answers to each question?*

6. *What actions would you take to address the school's priority need? Explain why.*

7. *How would you leverage the identified strength of the school to address the priority need?*

8. *What possible challenges might your actions create and what are some ways that you could manage these challenges?*

Kilo High School

Courtesy of littleny. Shutterstock

Mr. Reed, Principal
505 Students
170 Teachers

Kilo High School

Kilo High School has been identified by the State Education Department as a _persistently struggling_ school. The high school is located within a large metropolitan city. The school contains grades 9-12 with 505 students. The principal, Mr. Reed, was appointed two years ago; his three assistant principals each have over twelve years' experience. Mr. Reed's goal has been to remove Kilo High School from the State's _persistently struggling_ list. Thusly, Mr. Reed and his three assistant principals along with a recently established school governance committee have reviewed the school's data to identify the school's issues.

Discussion

The leadership characteristics and strategies used to facilitate the use of data at the school include:

- Establishing a clear vision for the use of data:
  Mr. Reed, principal, has a clear vision to remove his school from the State's _persistently struggling_ list. A school governance committee is involved in reviewing and refining the school's vision and support the use of data to drive instruction.
- Providing supports that promote a data-driven environment:
  The school governance committee and the assistant principals are the primary vehicle for providing support for data-driven instruction. With 33% of the teachers having a Master's Degree+30 credits and a large number of teachers rated effective and highly effective, the potential exists to harness these teachers' abilities to initiate a data-driven environment.
- Making data an ongoing part of the improvement process:

The principal is desirous of having his school removed from the State's *persistently struggling* list. However there are no supports in place other than the three assistant principals and the recently established school governance committee that might support the use of data as part of the improvement process.

- Creating a process or structure to analyze data:
  A process does exist for data analysis; the school has a governance committee which could take an active role in the use of data to inform practice.
- Teaching students to examine their own data:
  There are no mechanisms in place for students' to examine their own data to determine their next steps.
- Providing professional development on what the data tells you and how to use it:
  Table 1, indicates that the school has a staff of experienced teachers (33% have a Master's degree +30 credits) and no teachers are unqualified. Up to the present, teachers have not been involved in identifying their professional development needs for implementing data-driven instruction. Only school leaders have created a data-driven environment exclusive of teacher participation.
- Facilitating an organizational culture that supports data use for continuous improvement: The school governance committee serves as a first step to move the school away from dysfunction
- Providing teacher/data coach leadership: Although a school governance committee is in place, there are no lead teachers or data coaches identified to initiate data-driven professional development.

Table 1: Staffing

Principal	1
Assistant Principals	3
Total teachers	170
Teacher turnover rate	29%
Teachers teaching out of license	2%
Percent teachers with less than 3 years	3%
Percent teachers with Master's + 30	33%
Percent teachers not highly qualified	0%
Ineffective rating (number/%)	4/ 2%
Developing rating (number/%)	31/ 18%
Effective rating (number/%)	105/ 62%
Highly Effective rating (number/%)	30/ 18%

Table 2: Student Demographics

Total Pop.	Black	Hispanic	Asian	White	ELL	SWD	Suspensions	Attend.	Free/Red Lunch
505	285	125	11	84	34	115	18	78%	440
	56%	25%	2%	17%	7%	23%	3%		87%

Table 3: High School Completers

	Graduates + IEP	Regents Diploma		Adv. Regents Diploma		Non-Completers	
		Number	%	Number	%	Number	%
All Students	64	48	79	6	10	56	11
Gen Education	51	46	90	6	12	37	9
SWD	13	2	20	0	0	19	17

Table 4: Post-Graduation Plans of Completers

	Four year college		Two year college		Military		Employment		Unknown	
	#	%	#	%	#	%	#	%	#	%
All Students	0	0	49	77	0	0	15	23	0	0
Gen Education	0	0	40	78	0	0	11	22	0	0
SWD	0	0	9	69	0	0	4	31	0	0

Table 5a: History Regents Examination Results

	Global History and Geography				US History and Government			
		(Percent of students scoring at or above)				(Percent of students scoring at or above)		
	Total Tested	*55*	*65*	*85*	*Total Tested*	*55*	*65*	*85*
All Students	120	54	30	0	208	55	37	3
Gen Education	92	62	34	0	46	35	20	0
SWD	28	29	18	0	46	35	20	0
Asian	--	--	--	--	--	--	--	--
Black	75	49	28	0	124	48	34	2
Hispanic	28	57	36	0	45	69	44	4
White	--	--	--	--	--	--	--	--
ELL	--	--	--	--	5	40	40	0
Free/Red. Lunch	101	54	32	0	188	52	36	3

Table 5b: Science Regents Examination Results

	Living Environment				Earth Science			
		(Percent of students scoring at or above)				(Percent of students scoring at or above)		
	Total Tested	55	65	85	Total Tested	55	65	85
All Students	150	62	38	1	91	47	32	5
Gen Education	117	71	44	1	71	55	38	7
SWD	33	30	15	0	20	20	10	0
Asian	--	--	--	--	--	--	--	--
Black	96	61	36	0	56	41	25	2
Hispanic	37	62	38	0	19	53	37	11
White	--	--	--	--	16	63	50	13
ELL	12	25	0	0	--	--	--	--
Free/Red. Lunch	138	62	38	1	77	47	30	5

Table 5c: Mathematics Regents Examination Results

	Geometry				Trigonometry				Integrated Algebra			
		(Percent students scoring at or above)				(Percent students scoring at or above)				(Percent students scoring at or above)		
	Total Tested	55	65	85	Total Tested	55	65	85	Total Tested	55	65	85
All Students	100	31	15	1	38	24	21	3	239	48	23	0
Gen Education	77	32	19	1	--	--	--	--	179	55	26	0
SWD	23	26	0	0	--	--	--	--	60	28	13	0
Asian	--	--	--	--	--	--	--	--	--	--	--	--
Black	62	19	8	2	15	27	20	0	150	50	20	0
Hispanic	--	--	--	--	11	27	27	0	55	42	25	0
White	23	61	26	0	--	--	--	--	28	57	39	0
ELL	--	--	--	--	--	--	--	--	18	22	6	0
Free/Red. Lunch	85	28	13	0	29	24	21	0	212	48	30	0

Table 5d: Comprehensive English Regents

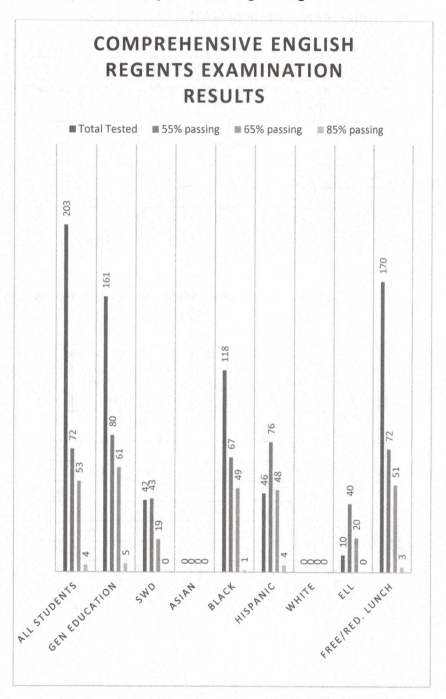

COMPREHENSIVE ENGLISH REGENTS EXAMINATION RESULTS

■ Total Tested ■ 55% passing ■ 65% passing ■ 85% passing

Table 6: New York State English as a Second Language Achievement Test (NYSESLAT)

Grade	Total Tested	Percent of Students Scoring at Level(s)			
		Beginning	Intermediate	Advanced	Proficient
9	21	43	33	24	0
10	5	20	0	40	40
11	--	--	--	--	--
12	--	--	--	--	--

Table 7: Accountability - Adequate Yearly Progress (AYP)

	English Language Arts			Mathematics		
	Made AYP	95% Tested	Safe Harbor	Made AYP	95% Tested	Safe Harbor
All Students	YES	YES	YES	NO	YES	NO
Asian	--	--	--	--	--	--
Black	NO	YES	NO	NO	YES	NO
Hispanic	--	--	--	--	--	--
White	--	--	--	--	--	--
SWD	--	--	--	--	--	--
ELL	--	--	--	--	--	--
Free/Red. Lunch	NO	YES	NO	NO	YES	NO

Table 8: Accountability for Graduation - Adequate Yearly Progress (AYP)

	Overall Graduation AYP	AYP Four Year Graduation Rate	AYP Five Year Graduation Rate
All Students	YES	NO	YES
Asian	--	--	--
Black	YES	NO	YES
Hispanic	YES	YES	YES
White	--	--	--
SWD	NO	NO	--
ELL	--	--	--
Free/Red. Lunch	YES	NO	YES

Selected Response:

1. All of the following issues are pressing needs at Kilo High School, except:
    - A. Turnover rate for teachers.
    - B. Average daily attendance for students.
    - C. Post-graduation plans to attend four year colleges.
    - D. Overall AYP Graduation Rate for the All Students subgroup.

2. Looking at Tables 5a, b, c, and d on Regents examination results, which statement is true?
    - A. A large number of students took the Trigonometry Regents successfully at the 85% level.
    - B. Students with Disabilities performed better than other subgroups on all Regents.
    - C. The Hispanic subgroup performed worse than Students with Disabilities on all Regents.

D. A small number in the All Students subgroup achieved 85% or better on the English Language Arts Regents.

3. In reviewing Tables 3 and 4, which of the following statements is NOT true:
   A. 11% of high school students did not graduate.
   B. More than 80% of High School Completers graduated with a Regents diploma.
   C. More graduating students attended two year colleges than four year colleges.
   D. There were less students graduating with an advanced Regents diploma than with a standard Regents diploma.

4. In examining teachers' staffing (Table 1) status, all the following are true, except:
   A. 80% of the teachers were APPR rated Effective or Highly Effective.
   B. There is a large percentage of teachers not highly qualified.
   C. 33% of the teaching staff have a Master's Degree+30 credits.
   D. There is a very small percentage of teachers teaching less than three years.

Performance Task:

1. Identify one strength of the school, citing evidence to support your response.

2. Identify three areas of need in the instructional program, citing evidence to support each need.

3. Which area of need would be your highest priority? Explain why.

4. What are two important questions you must answer to address your highest priority? Explain why each question is important to address.

5. How will you go about getting answers to each question?

6. What actions would you take to address the school's priority need? Explain why.
Actions to address priority need: Performance beyond expectation on Regents examinations.

7. How would you leverage the identified strength of the school to address the priority need?

8. What possible challenges might your actions create and what are some ways that you could manage these challenges?

The Lima
Preparatory School

Courtesy of longimanus. Shutterstock

467 Students
36 Teachers

The Lima Preparatory School

The Lima Preparatory School is a grade K-12 charter school located in a large metropolitan city. The school has been identified by the State Education Department as *persistently struggling*. There are 467 students, mostly coming from minority backgrounds, enrolled in the school. Students are required to take all state assessments and Regents. Although the school has been designated K-12, it currently has students in grades K-8. Parents participated in a selection process for admission into Lima Prep but are rarely involved in school activities. The principal who has been in her position for three years is supported by two assistant principals who mainly deal with disciplinary issues. The principal hardly leaves her office except when she has to evaluate her teaching staff. There are 36 teachers on staff with 13% teaching less than three years and 6% indicated as *not highly qualified*.

Discussion

The leadership characteristics and strategies used to facilitate the use of data at the school include:

- Establishing a clear vision for the use of data:
  The principal has been in this position for three years and achievement has not improved, in fact the school is designated *persistently struggling*. There is no vision for use of data. There is no evidence that the school has the capacity for developing effective and sustainable procedures for the use of data to improve instruction.
- Providing supports that promote a data-driven environment:
  Looking at the school's demographics and data, climate appears to be negative. With a 36% student suspension rate and no students performing at Levels 3+4, it is indicative of dysfunction as a result of a

disconnect between teaching and learning. Moreover with assistant principals constantly working on students' behavioral issues, there assistance in supporting instruction is non-existent. There are no other data-driven support mechanisms at the school.

- Making data an ongoing part of the improvement process:
  From the evidence provided, there is no use of data as any part of an improvement process. There's no school data committee; school leaders do not focus on data and teachers have not been part of any renewal process.
- Creating a process or structure to analyze data:
  There is no process or structures in place to examine and analyze data.
- Teaching students to examine their own data:
  There are no structures in place that facilitate students' use of their own data to develop next steps.
- Providing professional development on what the data tells you and how to use it:
  There is no plan to provide professional development for teachers in using data to improve teaching and learning. The assistant principals are only charged with maintaining order. The principal never leaves her office except to "write-up" teachers. Additionally, Table 1 points out that there is a constant yearly turnover of teachers.
- Facilitating an organizational culture that supports data use for continuous improvement:
  Looking at the data presented, the school overview and staffing patterns, it can be concluded is that the culture is negative and dysfunctional. The data indicates a high number of teacher turnovers, a high number of student suspensions, and a number of new teachers indicated as *not highly qualified*. Without

school leader support for improving teaching and learning, the culture remains toxic.

- Providing teacher/data coach leadership:
  There is no indication that there are lead teachers or data coaches on staff, both positions critical for initiating a renewal effort.

Table 1: Staffing

Principal	1
Assistant Principal	2
Total teachers	36
Teacher turnover rate	29%
Teachers teaching out of license	5%
Percent teachers with less than 3 years	13%
Percent teachers with Master's + 30	26%
Percent teachers not highly qualified	6%
Ineffective rating (number/%)	1/1%
Developing rating (number/%)	4/17%
Effective rating (number/%)	8/22%
Highly Effective rating (number/%)	23/60%

Table 2: Student Demographics

Total Pop.	Black	Hispanic	Asian	White	ELL	SWD	Suspensions	Attend.	Free/Red Lunch
	85%	7%	2%	5%	--	28%	36%	92%	87%
467	401	33	8	25	--	133	181		408

Table 3a: English Language Arts Achievement
Grades 3-5

	Grade 3: % scoring at level:					Grade 4: % scoring at level:					Grade 5: % scoring at level:				
	1	2	3	4	3+4	1	2	3	4	3+4	1	2	3	4	3+4
Statewide	37	31	27	4	31	30	39	21	9	30	36	36	21	9	30
All Students	71	29	0	0	0	86	14	0	0	0	81	15	3	0	3
Gen Education	70	30	0	0	0	87	13	0	0	0	100	0	0	0	0
SWD	80	20	0	0	0	84	16	0	0	0	84	14	2	0	2
Asian	--	--	--	--	--	--	--	--	--	--	--	--	--	--	--
Black	68	32	0	0	0	89	11	0	0	0	84	14	2	0	2
Hispanic	--	--	--	--	--	100	0	0	0	0	--	--	--	--	--
Poverty	74	26	0	0	0	86	14	0	0	0	83	15	2	0	2

Table 3b: English Language Arts Achievement
Grades 6-8

	Grade 6: % scoring at level:					Grade 7: % scoring at level:					Grade 8: % scoring at level:				
	1	2	3	4	3+4	1	2	3	4	3+4	1	2	3	4	3+4
Statewide	28	42	16	14	30	36	35	23	5	28	28	37	24	10	34
All Students	88	12	0	0	0	95	5	0	0	0	82	18	0	0	0
Gen Education	86	14	0	0	0	97	3	0	0	0	83	17	0	0	0
SWD	89	11	0	0	0	89	11	0	0	0	79	21	0	0	0
Asian	--	--	--	--	--	--	--	--	--	--	--	--	--	--	--
Black	89	11	0	0	0	94	6	0	0	0	84	16	0	0	0
Hispanic	--	--	--	--	--	--	--	--	--	--	--	--	--	--	--
Poverty	86	14	0	0	0	94	6	0	0	0	81	19	0	0	0

Table 4a: Mathematics Achievement
Grades 3-5

	Grade 3: % scoring at level					Grade 4: % scoring at level:					Grade 5: % scoring at level:				
	1	2	3	4	3+4	1	2	3	4	3+4	1	2	3	4	3+4
Statewide	28	32	24	16	40	27	31	24	18	42	32	29	24	15	39
All Students	54	46	0	0	0	86	14	0	0	0	77	23	0	0	0
Gen Education	57	43	0	0	0	87	13	0	0	0	70	30	0	0	0
SWD	40	60	0	0	0	83	17	0	0	0	94	6	0	0	0
Asian	--	--	--	--	--	--	--	--	--	--	--	--	--	--	--
Black	58	42	0	0	0	88	12	0	0	0	79	21	0	0	0
Hispanic	--	--	--	--	--	86	14	0	0	0	--	--	--	--	--
Poverty	57	43	0	0	0	88	12	0	0	0	93	7	0	0	0

Table 4b: Mathematics Achievement
Grades 6-8

	Grade 6: % scoring at level					Grade 7: % scoring at level:					Grade 8: % scoring at level:				
	1	2	3	4	3+4	1	2	3	4	3+4	1	2	3	4	3+4
Statewide	26	33	19	19	38	36	33	22	9	31	37	41	17	5	22
All Students	75	25	0	0	0	97	3	0	0	0	86	14	0	0	0
Gen Education	65	35	0	0	0	95	5	0	0	0	85	15	0	0	0
SWD	94	6	0	0	0	100	0	0	0	0	90	10	0	0	0
Asian	--	--	--	--	--	--	--	--	--	--	--	--	--	--	--
Black	76	24	0	0	0	98	2	0	0	0	89	11	0	0	0
Hispanic	--	--	--	--	--	--	--	--	--	--	--	--	--	--	--
Poverty	73	27	0	0	0	96	4	0	0	0	94	16	0	0	0

Table 5: Science Achievement
Grades 4 and 8

	4th Grade % scoring at level:					8th Grade % scoring at level:				
	1	2	3	4	3+4	1	2	3	4	3+4
Statewide	3	10	34	53	87	8	23	40	28	68
All Students	29	35	35	2	37	56	41	4	0	4
Gen Education	29	37	34	0	34	55	43	3	0	3
SWD	29	29	35	6	41	57	36	7	0	7
Asian	--	--	--	--	--	--	--	--	--	--
Black	39	27	34	0	34	62	36	2	0	2
Hispanic	0	71	29	0	29	--	--	--	--	--
Poverty	30	34	34	2	36	59	38	3	0	3

Table 6: Regents Examination Results
Grade 8

	Integrated Algebra (Percent of students scoring at or above)			
	Total Tested	55	65	85
All Students	9	89	67	0
Gen Education	9	89	67	0
SWD	--	--	--	--
Asian	--	--	--	--
Black	--	--	--	--
Hispanic	--	--	--	--
Poverty	--	--	--	--

Table 7a: Middle Level English Language Arts and Mathematics Results Accountability Adequate Yearly Progress (AYP)

	English Language Arts			Mathematics		
	Made AYP	Tested 95%	Safe Harbor	Made AYP	Tested 95%	Safe Harbor
All Students	NO	YES	NO	NO	YES	NO
SWD	NO	NO	NO	NO	NO	NO
Asian	--	--	--	--	--	--
Black	NO	YES	NO	NO	YES	NO
Hispanic	--	--	--	--	--	--
Poverty	NO	YES	NO	NO	YES	NO

Table 7b: Middle Level Science Results Accountability Adequate Yearly Progress (AYP)

	Science		
	Made AYP	Tested 95%	Safe Harbor
All Students	NO	YES	NO
SWD	--	--	--
Asian	--	--	--
Black	NO	YES	NO
Hispanic	--	--	--
Poverty	NO	YES	NO

Selected Response:

1. The principal of the The Lima Preparatory School reviewed the data and concluded:

> *A. Although most teachers were rated Highly Effective and Effective, student achievement was low.*

125

B. Student suspension is not an area of concern.
C. The performance of the various subgroups was acceptable.
D. The principal does not need to expend time and energy on teachers rated as Ineffective and Developing.

2. In looking carefully at the English Language Arts and Mathematics assessment results (Tables 3a & 3b), the principal concluded:
   A. The All Students subgroup in grades 3 through 8 performed consistently above the statewide average as evidenced by their Level 3+4 scores.
   B. The All Students subgroup in grades 3 through 8 performed consistently below the statewide average as evidenced by their Level 3+4 scores.
   C. The Black, SWDs and Poverty subgroups scored above the statewide average on the Grade 5 Mathematics Assessment.
   D. There were students in each subgroup who achieved at performance level 3 on all English Language Arts examinations.

3. In looking carefully at Science Grade 4 and 8 assessment results (Table 5) the principal made the following observation:
   A. The All Students subgroup performed consistently above the statewide average.
   B. Students' performance in Grade 8 was far better than their performance in Grade 4.
   C. Students' performance in Grade 4 was far better than their performance in Grade 8.
   D. The Asian subgroup performed consistently above the statewide average on Level 3+4 on Grade 4 and Grade 8.

4. Looking at Table 7a and 7b, Accountability – Adequate Yearly Progress for The Lima Preparatory School, which of the following statements is correct:

> *A. The Asian and Hispanic subgroups made AYP for English Language Arts and Mathematics.*
> *B. All subgroups achieved at Safe Harbor levels.*
> *C. The All Students subgroup made Safe Harbor for English Language Arts, Mathematics and Science.*
> *D. The All Students subgroup made AYP in English Language Arts, Mathematics and Science.*

Performance Task:

1. What are two primary issues presented by the data and why do you believe it to be so?

2. What are two important questions you must address as principal to explore this issue? Explain why each question is important?

3. How will you go about getting answers to each question? What challenges might you face in getting answers to your questions?

4. Describe one possible finding of your inquiry process and the potential action that finding would imply.

Answers

Alpha Junior High School

1. B
2. A
3. B
4. C

Performance Task:

1. Give one strength of Alpha Junior High School. What evidence would you use to support this determination? What strategy might you use to enhance this strength?
Strength:

- Level 3+4 performance of the All Students subgroup above statewide scoring level in Grade 7 English Language Arts and Mathematics and for Grade 8 English Language Arts for two consecutive years.
  Evidence: Tables 3, 4, 5 and 6.
- Performance for subgroups General Education, Asian, Black, Hispanic and Poverty above the Statewide scoring level in Grade 7 English Language Arts and Mathematics and for Grade 8 English Language Arts.
  Evidence: Tables 3, 4, 5, and 6.

Strategy:

- Support this strength by setting up a data committee to examine the school's effectiveness so that teachers could build on strengths to address areas of concern.

2. List three areas of need for Alpha Junior High School. What evidence would you use to support this determination?

129

Areas of need:

- *Grade 8 Mathematics for the current year is below the statewide average for all subgroups except Asians.*
  Evidence: Table 5
- *9% suspension rate*
  Evidence: Table 2
- *Low achievement (below statewide levels of performance) for SWDs in English Language Arts grades 7 and 8 and Mathematics grades 7 and 8 for previous year and current year.*
  Evidence: Tables 3, 4, 5, and 6
- *The disparity between students' test scores and the highly effective rating of the staff. According to Table 1, no one on staff is considered unqualified. However, student achievement results, as indicated in Tables 3 through 8, evidence that some subgroups are struggling academically. (Support: Decrease in achievement scores (Level 3+4) from the previous year to the current year in English Language Arts and Mathematics across grades 7 and 8.*
  Evidence: Tables 3, 4, 5, and 6

3. Which area of need would be your highest priority? Explain why.

Highest priority need:

- *Improving achievement for SWDs since they perform significantly lower than the statewide average.*

Explanation: By addressing this achievement gap successfully, the overall school achievement would skyrocket. Moreover, this is the neediest cohort in the school which may have been historically underserved in a separate setting.

4. What are two important questions you must answer to address your highest priority? Explain why each question is important to address.

Two important questions:

- *Why are performance scores for SWDs significantly lower than other subgroups?*

Explanation: It is important to address this question because current instructional strategies are not meeting the need of this subgroup.

- *Why didn't the SWDs subgroup make Adequate Yearly Progress in Mathematics?*

Explanation: It is important to address because by examining this critical issue will shed light on this subgroup's lack of success in Mathematics and perhaps lead to enacting more effective instructional strategies.

5. How would you go about getting answers to each question?

Getting the answer to the first question:

- *Establish a data committee comprised of the various constituencies within the school community and to include general education and special education teachers, parents, principal or assistant principal. This committee would delve into reasons for SWDs underachievement by analyzing formative and summative data.*

Getting the answer to the second question:

- *Use the data committee already established to examine the process for achieving Adequate Yearly Progress, identifying the factors attributed to this low score and how the committee might ascertain pathways for remediation.*

6. What actions would you take to address the school's priority need? Explain why.

Actions:

- *The data committee could suggest several simultaneous pathways, including establishing professional learning communities for special education and general education teachers to develop more effective teaching practices.*
- *A second pathway could include establishing a mentoring program for either special or general education teachers having difficulties implementing new differentiated instructional strategies.*
- *A third pathway might include establishing a professional development program.*
- *A fourth pathway could include reaching out to schools having similar issues so that similar strategies might be applied to Alpha Junior High School.*

Explanation: The goal of these multiple pathways is to improve academic performance for SWDs.

7. How would you leverage the identified strength of the school to address the priority need?

Leveraging strength:

- *Alpha Junior High School evidences effective instruction for general education students as well as for most subgroups. The principal should leverage this strength to apply these positive outcomes towards improving teaching and learning for SWDs.*

8. What possible challenges might your actions create and what are some ways that you could manage these challenges?

Challenges:

- *A possible challenge might include teachers' negative feelings about SWDs*

- *Teacher preparation for teaching a difficult student population having a variety of learning issues.*

Management:

- *Through planned professional development to enhance practice and foster collaboration between general and special education teachers, more positive learning expectations could be developed.*
- *By establishing professional learning communities, teachers would be afforded opportunities to address common issues through collegiality to meet the learning needs of these subgroups.*

Bravo Academy

Selected Response:
1. A
2. B
3. D
4. D

Performance Task:
1. *What are two primary issues presented by the data and why do you believe it to be so?*
Primary issues:

- *Consistent poor performance of SWDs below the statewide average for English Language Arts in Grades 3, 4 and 5. Table 3 identifies the SWDs subgroup in grades 3, 4 and 5 consistently performing below the statewide average.*

- *Consistent poor performance of SWDs below the statewide average for Mathematics in Grades 3, 4 and 5. Table 4 identifies the SWDs subgroup in grades 3, 4 and 5 consistently performing below the statewide average.*

- *Poor performance for the Hispanic subgroup below the statewide average on the English Language Arts assessment in grades 4 and 5. Table 3 corroborates this finding.*

- *Poor performance for the Hispanic subgroup below the statewide average on the Mathematics assessment in grades 3 and 4. Table 4 corroborates this finding.*

Explanation: Poor performance could be related to the lack of preparation and confidence in teaching special populations.

2. *What are two important questions you must address as principal to explore this issue? Explain why each question is important?*

Two important questions:

- *Why are children classified as special education having consistent difficulties achieving in English Language Arts and Mathematics? Tables 3 and 4 point consistently to SWDs underperforming in English Language Arts and Mathematics in grades 3, 4, and 5.*

Explanation: By identifying and remediating this low achieving subgroup, improved achievement will have a spillover to all other subgroups as instructional strategies better meet the needs of all learners.

- *What is the level of preparedness for teachers teaching SWDs?*

Explanation: It is important to identify and ameliorate lapses in good instructional practice. SWDs lack of achievement might be attributed to teachers' discomfort implementing differentiated instructional strategies to meet the needs of this subgroup.

3. *How will you go about getting answers to each question? What challenges might you face in getting answers to your questions?*

Getting the answer to the first question:

- *It will be necessary to establish a task force consisting of highly effective general and special educators to investigate successful instructional strategies that meets the needs of SWDs. This task force will set up various subcommittees to examine formative and summative data, instructional strategies and visiting effective programs at neighboring schools.*

135

Challenge: Teachers could be reluctant to volunteer and participate in the task force or serve on subcommittees.

Getting the answers the second question:

- *Establish a separate task force on professional development. 70% of the teachers have a master's degree; 97% of the teachers are rated effective or highly effective. This data could lead to the conclusion that teachers might not be on-board with the need for additional professional development for SWDs learners.*

Challenge: Teachers might be reluctant to volunteer and participate in the task force or serve on committees because of their seniority and high performance rating. They might not see the need for additional instructional strategies such as, differentiated instruction.

4. Describe one possible finding of your inquiry process and the potential action that finding would imply.
Finding:

- *Teachers have insufficient skills to teach SWDs.*

Action:

- *Initiate a professional development program for teachers to acquire those skills. Additionally, it might be difficult for teachers to accept the fact that they are less than effective in meeting the learning needs of SWDs and therefore resistant to change. Teacher leaders would have to step forward to encourage and facilitate colleagues' participation in professional learning opportunities to enhance their teaching methodologies for the SWDs population. By establishing professional learning communities and validating leader leadership positions, the school can address these inadequacies.*

Charlie High School

Selected Response:
1. B
2. B
3. C
4. B

Performance Task:

1. Identify one strength of the school, citing evidence to support your response.

Strengths for Charlie High School:

- *97% of staff are rated effective or highly effective Evidence: Table 1: 69% effective, 30% highly effective*

- *85% of all students received a Regents diploma. Evidence: Table 3: 85% all students received a Regents diploma*

- *The high school has a diverse school population Evidence: Table 2: indicates 29% Black, 41% Hispanic, 7% Asian, 26% White*

- *74% of graduates went to either two or four year college. Evidence: Table 4: 47% attended a four year college; 27% attended a two year college*

- *Regents performance: ELA-74%, Algebra-68%, Global History-57%, US History-77%, Living Environment-64%, Earth Science 53%, Geometry-54%, Trigonometry-63% of all students received a 65 or greater. Evidence: Tables 5a, 5b, 5c, 5d: Regents performance*

- *All students made Annual Yearly Progress for the four and five year graduation rate*

- *Evidence: (Table 7: Graduation Rate for Accountability*

2. Identify three areas of need in the instructional program, citing evidence to support each need.
Areas of need:
- *High school completion low for SWDs.*
  Evidence: Table 3: Only 25% of SWDs received a Regents diploma
- *Post-graduation plans for SWDs are problematic. Evidence: Table 4: Only 17% plan on attending a four year college and 22% on attending a two year college.*
- *Performance on Regents for SWDs.*
  Evidence: Table 5 a, b, c, d: Across the board SWDs performed poorly as compared to general education students.
- *Performance on Regents in the 85% range for all students:*
  Evidence: Table 5 a, b, c, d: Across all subject areas student performance is low at the 85% cut score
- *Performance on Regents for ELL.*
  Evidence: Table 5 a, b, c, d: ELL performed poorly on ELA, Global History, US History, and Living Environment.
- *All Students, SWDs, Black, Free & Reduced Lunch subgroups did not make Adequate Yearly Progress in ELA.*
  Evidence: Table 6: Accountability indicates non-performing subgroups.
- *All Students, SWDs, Free & Reduced Lunch subgroups did not make Adequate Yearly Progress in Mathematics.*
  Evidence: Table 6 Accountability indicates non-performing subgroups.

- *Four and Five Year Graduation Rate for Hispanic and Black subgroups.*
  Evidence: Table 7 Graduation Rate Accountability shows that Hispanics did not make AYP in four year graduation rate; Blacks did not make AYP in the five year graduation rate.

3. *Which area of need would be your highest priority? Explain why.*
Highest priority need:
   - *Underperformance in English Language Arts and Mathematics for SWDs and Hispanic subgroups.*
   Explanation: Lower performance on Regents examinations (Tables 5 a, b, c, d). However, with SWDs and Hispanic subgroups underperforming, 99% of the teachers were rated effective or highly effective. This seems to be a problematic.

4. *What are two important questions you must answer to address your highest priority? Explain why each question is important to address.*
Important questions:
   - *Why are SWDs underperforming?*
   Explanation: It is important to address this question because finding the answer will improve the AYP and Graduation rate of these subgroups.
   - *Why is the Hispanic subgroup underperforming?*
   Explanation: It is important to address this issue because curricular modifications are necessary to meet the needs of this subgroup performance. It is also important to identify if some of the Hispanic subgroup English Language Learners.

5. *How will you go about getting answers to each question?*

Getting the answers to the first question:

- *Set up a committee of general and special education teachers and including assistant principals to examine why there is a lag in achievement for SWDs. The committee would look at: SWDs achievement over time, teaching and learning strategies, scheduling, areas of successful practice and similar high schools that have experience in reducing the achievement gap for the SWDs subgroup.*

Getting the answers to the second question:

- *Collaboratively working with the district Supervisor for Second Language Programs, set up a committee to investigate issues around the lower achievement rate for the Hispanic subgroup. This committee would look at teaching and learning strategies, scheduling, areas of successful practice and at similar high schools that have successful experience dealing with this subgroup.*

6. What actions would you take to address the school's priority need? Explain why.
Actions:

- *The underperformance of SWDs and Hispanic subgroups requires the following actions to address this top priority need:*
  - *Establish a task force including District Supervisors, building assistant principals and teachers to address each academic issue.*
  - *Conduct Inter-visitations to schools with successful programs for SWDs and Hispanic subgroups.*
  - *Meet with community based organizations, local colleges, teachers' union representatives and families of SWDs and Hispanic subgroups to get their input.*

141

- *Meet with the superintendent and/or assistant superintendent for their input.*

Explanation: These actions imply a collaborative effort to bring about change in student performance.

7. How would you leverage the identified strength of the school to address the priority need?

Leveraging strength:

- *Charlie High School has experienced success in meeting the needs of general education students as well as some of its constituent subgroups. In Identifying those teachers using successful teaching and learning strategies, they could be transported to successfully deal with learning strategies for SWDs and Hispanic subgroups. Since 99% of the teaching staff has been rated effective or highly effective, there must be a cadre of teachers available to become teacher leaders to address these needs.*

8. What possible challenges might your actions create and what are some ways that you could manage these challenges?

Challenges:

- *A significant challenge might be resistance to change that goes along with having a majority of teachers (58%) being senor having a Master's degree + 30 credits.*
- *Some teachers are set in their expectations for learning; they need to become more amenable to change.*

Management:

- *By initiating opportunities for leadership, these teacher leaders could support the school's effort to strengthen instructional rigor for the SWDs and*

Hispanic subgroups. Teacher leaders could facilitate professional development to deal with achievement for SWDs and Hispanic subgroups.

Delta Middle School

1. C
2. A
3. B
4. C

Performance Task:

1. What are two primary issues presented in this scenario, and why do you believe this to be so?

Primary issues:

- *High number of students classified as SWDs*
- *Underachievement of SWDs in English Language Arts and Mathematics on State assessments*
- *All Students, White and SWDs subgroups did not make AYP for Mathematics*

Explanation: 75% of the teachers have a Master's degree + 30 credits which indicates that the staff is senior. They might be complacent in their teaching practice and/or resistant to modify their instructional practices for SWDs and other subgroups. Likewise, lower performance by Black and Hispanic subgroups in Levels 3+4 might also be attributed to a lack of differentiated instructional strategies to meet the needs of these subgroups' learning styles.

2. What are two important questions you must address in order to explore this issue? Explain why each is important to address.

Important questions:

- *Why are there great numbers of students classified as SWDs?*

144

Importance: An investigation into students' classifications might reveal the need for teachers' professional development.

- *Although the school is high achieving, several subgroups are not performing equally as well. What might this be attributed to?*

Explanation: Looking at performance data for subgroups could reveal that additional professional development might be necessary because differentiated teaching strategies for diversified learners is lacking.

3. How will you go about getting answers to each question? What challenges might you face in getting answers to your questions?

Getting answers to the first question:

- *Establish a task force to investigate why the school has an excessive classification rate for youngsters requiring special educational services. Task force members should include general and special educators, an assistant principal, a special education supervisor, and possibly the district Director of Special Education. The task force should review, referrals disaggregating them by disability. The task force should also review instructional strategies used throughout the school for SWDs and general education students whose performance levels have not be satisfactory to determine if these activities meet the needs of diverse learners.*

Challenge: Teacher willingness to participate in such a task force might be in doubt especially when investigating practice of their colleagues.

Getting answers to the second question:

- *Have data committee review subgroup performance and which teachers were successful in teaching classified youngsters. The committee could then look at those effective practices for sharing among the staff.*

Challenge: Teacher willingness to investigate practice of their peers could come into question.

4. Describe one possible finding of your inquiry process and the potential action that finding would imply.

Findings:

- *Teachers haven't participated in a professional development program, for example: differentiating instruction for special populations.*
- *Teachers may not be using RtI (Response to Intervention) strategies in their classrooms.*

Actions:

- *Initiate a multi-pronged professional development initiative for all teachers to familiarize them with successful instructional strategies for special education students.*
- *At the same time provide staff training in Response to Intervention (RtI) strategies.*
- *Arrange for inter-visitation of schools that successfully use these strategies throughout their classrooms.*

Echo Alternative High School

Selected Response:
1. B
2. D
3. D
4. C

Performance Task:

1. Identify one strength of this school, citing evidence to support your response.

Strengths:
- Clearly the graduation rate for this difficult population including minority students who are over-age and under-credited is a strength.
- Collaborative culture: school leaders and teachers work together to meet the needs of this difficult student population.

Evidence:
- 93% (or 88) of the All Students subgroup graduated with a Regents diploma. Additionally the Four Year Accountability Rate for the All Students subgroup as well as for Black and Hispanic subgroups show that the school has surpassed the "Progress Target" as identified by the State Education Department.
- The data team is led by teachers; the school has teacher data coach; both circumstances have facilitated achievement beyond expectation.

2. Identify three areas of need in the instructional program, citing evidence to support each need.

Areas of need:
- Performance on Regents examinations at 85% and above is lacking for the All Students subgroup as well as for other subgroups.

Evidence: Tables 5a, b, c and d.

- *Post-graduation plans indicates that only 7% of the All Students subgroup planned to attend a four year college. 75% planned to intend to attend a two year college.*
Evidence: Table 4 also indicates that SWDs did not intend to pursue a four year college education and only eight wanted to pursue a two year college education.
- *There is a 21% high school non-completion rate for all students.*
Evidence: Table 3.
- *The Hispanic and the Free/Reduced Lunch subgroups did not make AYP for English Language Arts and Mathematics. The Black subgroup did not make AYP for Mathematics. Likewise the All Students subgroup did not make AYP for Mathematics.*
Evidence: Table 6, Adequate Yearly Progress indicates a lack of Adequate Yearly Progress for subgroups.

3. Which area of need would be your highest priority? Explain.

Highest priority need:

- *Not making Adequate Yearly Progress in English Language Arts and for Mathematics.*

Explanation: Instruction is less than optimal in English Language Arts and Mathematics. An intervening variable which probably effects this outcome is that 31% of teachers were rated as developing. In order for this high school to move towards higher achieving levels, effective teachers must be identified that use a variety of instructional strategies to meet needs of disenfranchised students. Identified underperforming teachers should be provided opportunities to

148

collaborate with highly effective teachers. If basic instruction is improved, then performance on Regents examinations, graduation rate and attendance at four year colleges will improve.

4. What are two important questions you must answer to address your highest priority area of need? Explain why each question is important to address. Must relate to Q3. Important questions:

- *Why did the school not make Adequate Yearly Progress in English Language Arts and Mathematics?*

Explanation: It is crucial for the school to determine this area of need in order for the   school to advance its graduation rate and improve instruction for subgroups.

- *Why did the school have a large number of developing teachers?*

Explanation: It is important to determine the relationship of poor teaching to student success so that appropriate instructional goals could be put into place to improve and raise student achievement.

5. How will you go about getting answers to EACH question?
Getting the answer to the first question:

- *The school data committee is a good mechanism to get various constituents to the table to jointly investigate the issue regarding not making Adequate Yearly Progress.*

Getting the answer to the second question:

- *School leaders and the data coach should look at the preparation of developing and ineffective rated teachers to jointly decide what professional development would be most effective to improve their skills.*

6. *What actions would you take to address the school's priority need? Explain why. Refer to Q3.*

Actions: In order to address this need and to improve teaching and learning in English Language Arts and Mathematics for all teachers:

- *Organize professional development around English Language Arts and Mathematics stressing strategies that work with difficult populations (from committee work).*
- *Organize and schedule inter-visitations to similar schools that have successfully addressed English Language Arts and Mathematics achievement gaps.*
- *Institute an in-service program taught by peer teachers demonstrating exemplary practice in English Language Arts and Mathematics.*
- *Arrange for classroom inter-visitations with teachers' whose practice is exemplary.*
- *Invite the services of a proven and successful consultants in English Language Arts and Mathematics (upon agreement with the data committee)*

Explanation: To improve English Language Arts and Mathematics instruction, teachers' abilities to teach this challenging population must be addressed. Teachers need to develop differentiated instructional strategies so that their learners experience success.

7. *How would you leverage the identified strength of the school to address the priority need? Refer to Q1.*

Strength: The high school graduation for minority students who are over-age and under-credited is a strength. 93% (or 88) of the All Students subgroup graduated with a Regents diploma.

Leveraging strength:

- *This strength implies that there are a number of teachers evidencing human capital success towards the acquisition of instructional teaching strategies for difficult students. Using these teachers as models and mentors for lesser achieving colleagues would leverage achievement to ever-increasing numbers. Lesser achieving teachers could work in professional learning communities with highly effective teachers to replicate the latter's classroom successes.*

8. What possible challenges might your actions create and what are some ways that you could manage these challenges? Refer toQ6.

Challenges:

- *The major challenge to improving instruction is teachers' resistance to change and participation in professional development that they believe is not necessary.*
- *Teachers may not see the need to modify practice because they have always taught that way. It's the students' problems for not learning. This adage is not productive for academic success for this school population. Teachers need to constantly modify practice and differentiate instruction to support the varied learning styles of their students.*

Management:

- *To effectively manage resistance to change requires a shift in the school's culture to make those less than effective teachers will participants in improvement. It implies that those teachers need to recognize their ineffectiveness and want to develop pathways to improvement. Schools leaders need to be supportive of this process for it to take hold within the school.*

- *The school's data coach could be instrumental in assisting with modeling successful instructional practices and arranging for inter-visitation for developing and ineffective teachers.*

Foxtrot Elementary School

Selected Response:
1. D
2. C
3. A
4. C

Performance Task:

1. Identify one strength of the school, citing evidence to support your response.

Strengths:

- *Black, Hispanic and Free/Reduced Lunch subgroups have made Adequate Yearly Progress in English Language Arts and Mathematics.*
  Evidence: Table 5 clearly indicates the achievement levels of these subgroups.

- *There is a low suspension rate, 1% or 5 students and a fairly high average daily attendance of 93%.*
  Evidence: Table 2.

- *88% of its teachers are identified as "Effective."*
  Evidence: Table 1.

2. Identify three areas of need in the instructional program, citing evidence to support each need.

Areas of need:

- *There is a high turnover rate among the teaching staff, 17%.*
  Evidence: Table 1. (Although in some circumstances this might be strength.)

- *Students consistently perform below the statewide average in English Language Arts and Mathematics for Grades 3, 4 and 5.*
  Evidence: Table 3.

- The SWDs subgroup consistently performs below the statewide average in English Language Arts and Mathematics and below the average of any other subgroup.
  Evidence: Table 3.
- The school did not make Adequate Yearly Progress for All Students in English Language Arts and for SWDs in English Language Arts and Mathematics.
  Evidence: Table 5.

3. Which area of need would be your highest priority? Explain why.
Highest priority need:
- The highest priority would be that the All Students subgroup exhibits scores below the statewide average in English Language Arts and Mathematics.

Explanation: This indicates that teachers need to improve students' academic achievement in those areas so that all subgroups would likewise improve performance. This is directly related to implementing differentiated instructional strategies to meet the needs of diverse learners. Although 88% of the teachers have been rated "effective," it is apparent that they lack the skills needed to improve subgroup performance.

4. What are two important questions you must answer to address your highest priority? Explain why each question is important to address.
Important questions:
- Is there a disconnect with teachers' performance (88% effective) and the achievement performance of student subgroups in English Language Arts and Mathematics?

154

Explanation: This question is important to understand why the achievement gap exists and why teachers' are not successfully addressing the issue of student achievement.

- *What should the principal do to address the issue of low student performance?*

Explanation: This question is important because it will help to clarify the renewal process and the roles of participants to effectively implement change.

5. How will you go about getting answers to each question?

Getting the answer to the first question:

- *Disconnect with teacher performance and student achievement:*
  Establish a task force and/or empower the data team to identify teachers who have successfully dealt with the achievement of subgroups to develop pathways to inform instruction for colleagues.

Getting the answer to the second question:

- *Teacher and student low performance:*
  Use the structures in place to address low performance, namely grade leaders' should work with their underperforming colleagues, the data team should identify successful instructional strategies and the professional development committee should outline a plan for ongoing learning.

6. What actions would you take to address the school's priority need? Explain why.

Actions:

- *In order to reduce the achievement gap for subgroups, operationalize the recommendations of the task force/data team.*

155

- *Expand professional development.*
- *Support inter-visitation to other schools that have reduced the achievement gap.*
- *Implement professional learning communities to enhance collaboration.*
- *Use grade leaders as instructional coaches to guide and support teachers to adopt differentiating instructional opportunities for all students.*

Explanation: All these suggestions will facilitate reduction of the achievement gap for subgroups by strengthening the instructional program.

7. How would you leverage the identified strength of the school to address the priority need?
Leveraging strength:
- *Experienced teachers can form a core group (professional learning community) to facilitate the change process. Clearly since the Black and Hispanic subgroups have made Adequate Yearly Progress, there is a cadre of instructionally effective teachers that can share their successes.*

8. What possible challenges might your actions create and what are some ways that you could manage these challenges?
Challenges:
- *Change is difficult to be accepted by some experienced teachers. The research indicates that resistance to change can cause a staff to be frozen in place, unable to address change because of their resistance to "new ideas."*
- *Teachers may be satisfied with the status quo, not interested in grade leaders' efforts to change instructional practice.*

- *Teachers may not want to participate on the data team and school governance committee because of the commitment of time.*

Management:

- *To manage these challenges, it will be necessary to reduce teacher resistance to change by working with willing participants and supporting those teachers willing to change their practice by offering incentives to become part of the change process. Extra and/or common preparation time and additional resources might be offered. Additionally, grade leaders serving as instructional coaches might further support the change process.*

Gulf Elementary School

Selected Response:
1. C
2. B
3. D
4. B

Performance Task:
1. What are two primary issues presented in this scenario, and why do you believe this to be so?
Primary issues:

- Achievement for SWDs
Importance: SWDs are consistently performing below their peers at Level 3+4 and below the statewide average in English Language Arts.
Evidence: Table 3 and 4

- The high percent of classified children
Importance: For a high achieving school with only 339 students, 40 students (12%) classified is significant.
Evidence: Table 2

- The high number of senior staff and the underachievement of the SWDs subgroup.
Evidence: Table 1 indicates that 81% of the teachers possess a Master's Degree + 30 credits. Table 1 indicates that all teachers were rated Effective and Highly Effective.

Explanation: This could be a professional development issue since experienced and highly rated teachers might have experience difficulty in teaching subgroups such as SWDs

2. What are two important questions you must address in order to explore this issue? Explain why each is important to address.

Important questions:

- *Is there a correlation of teacher performance ratings with academic achievement of SWDs?*

Explanation: This investigation would yield the necessity for additional training for teachers to differentiate instruction for SWDs.

- *Why were all teachers rated Effective or Highly Effective?*

Explanation: In examining teacher evaluation, the principal might obtain information that would form the basis for restructuring her instructional goals for subgroups for the following year.

3. How will you go about getting answers to each question? What challenges might you face in getting answers to your questions?

Getting the answer to the first question:

- *Initiate a task force of special and regular educators, members of the support team, and the principal to investigate why the discrepant learning for classified children.*

    Challenge: A potential challenge might include resistance to examine colleagues teaching and learning strategies. "if it ain't broke, don't fix it" mentality.

Getting the answer to the second question:

- *Initiate a conversation with fellow principals from other district elementary schools, looking at their rationale for rating teachers. At the same time, look at the State Education Department web site to examine ratings of similar schools across the region. Finally discuss with the superintendent/ assistant superintendent the rationale for the rating process across the district.*

Challenges: Colleagues might not be forthcoming about their rating rationale. Moreover, in the conversation with the superintendent or assistant superintendent asking about the efficacy of the rating system might not a worthwhile effort especially since the rating system was negotiated by union and district.

4. Describe one possible finding of your inquiry process and the potential action that finding would imply.
Finding:
- *The need for professional development to provide classroom teachers with instructional strategies to enhance SWDs achievement.*

Action:
- *Ongoing professional development including a timeframe for implementation, proposed activities, schedule for follow-up including walk-throughs to observe implementation of learnings and an assessment process to measure effectiveness.*

Hotel Middle School

1. A
2. C
3. D
4. D

1. *Give one strength of Hotel Middle School. What evidence would you use to support this determination? What strategy might you use to enhance this strength?*
Strengths:

- *Consistent achievement for All Students above the statewide average in English Language Arts and Mathematics for grades 6, 7, and 8.*
  Evidence: Tables 3 and 4.
  Enhancement strategy: Provide rewards for consistent achievement above expectation; for students certificates and emails to parents; for teachers certificates, emails or celebrations with food (e.g. breakfasts)
- *Implementation of a number of Regents high school level classes in Science and Mathematics (Integrated Algebra, Geometry, Earth Science, and Living Environment)*
  Evidence: Tables 5, 6, and 7.
  Enhancement Strategy: Recognize teachers, parents, and students for their advanced scholarship.
- *Consistently attaining Adequate Yearly Progress for the All Students subgroup as well as for all subgroups.*

161

Evidence: Table 8.
Enhancement Strategy: Provide positive reinforcement for teachers, parents, and students. Blogging, Emailing, Certificates, Celebrations.

- *100% of the staff received a highly effective or effective rating.*
  Evidence: Table 1.
  Enhancement Strategy: Staff recognition via email, letters or certificates, and celebrations (with food)

2. List three areas of need for Hotel Middle School. What evidence would you use to support this determination?
Areas of need:

- *Student achievement for SWDs, Hispanic, and (sometimes Black) subgroups.*
  Evidence: Tables 3, 4, and 5 indicate lower performance for these subgroups on English Language Arts, Mathematics, and Science examinations.
- *Performance beyond expectation on Algebra, Geometry, Earth Science, and Living Environment Regents for minority subgroups is almost non-existent.*
  Evidence: Tables 5, 6, and 7 indicate performance on Regents examinations for subgroups is below the All Students subgroup and General Education subgroup.
- *The performance of SWDs subgroup is below other subgroups on the 8th Science examination.*
  Evidence: Table 5 indicates below average performance of the SWDs subgroup compared to the All Students subgroup.
- *100% of the teaching staff received an effective or highly effective rating, yet performance of minority subgroups on State examinations was lower than the All Students subgroup.*

Table 1 Staff indicates 100% of staff is effective or highly effective. Tables 3 and 4 show results in English Language Arts and Mathematics by subgroup.

3. Which area of need would be your highest priority? Explain why.
Highest priority need:
- Student achievement for SWDs, Hispanic, and (sometimes Black) subgroups is below the statewide average.

Explanation: As indicated, Tables 3, 4, and 5 demonstrate lower performance on English Language Arts, Mathematics, and Science examinations for these subgroups. Subgroup achievement is incongruent with teacher ratings. For a school to be functioning in a highly effective manner, all students must be performing at Level 3 or 4.

4. What are two important questions you must answer to address your highest priority? Explain why each question is important to address.
Important questions:
- Why are subgroups underperforming?

Explanation: It is important to analyze why subgroups are underperforming so that instruction can be modified and differentiated to meet the needs of these subgroups.

- Why are 100% of teachers rated effective or highly effective?

Explanation: It is important to understand the criteria for rating teachers so that modifications to the rating system include teaching and learning strategies to improve performance.

5. *How would you go about getting answers to each question?*
Getting the answer to the first question:
- *Establish a task force or committee to examine the data regarding performance of subgroups. The task force would include representatives of various constituencies, e.g. reading teachers, classroom teachers, special educators, assistant principal, district personnel, parents, and community members.*

Getting the answer to the second question:
- *Discuss with the superintendent or assistant superintendent the teacher evaluation system. Likewise ask fellow principals within the school district how the rating system was established, criteria for evaluation, and how their teachers' were rated.*

6. *What actions would you take to address the school's priority need? Explain why.*
Actions:
- *Establish a committee to address minority subgroup achievement (Hispanic, Black, SWDs)*
- *Establish an audit committee to perform an audit of the instructional program, examining how it meets the needs of these subgroups.*
- *Examine the past and current professional development offerings to see if they address the needs of these subgroups.*
- *Initiate and implement a professional development program to address audited needs.*

Explanation: By involving teacher input in determining subgroup performance, teachers will assume greater responsibility for modifying instructional practice.

7. How would you leverage the identified strength of the school to address the priority need?
Leveraging strength:

- *Since there is a significant number of teachers rated highly effective (69% or 20 teachers), these highly effective experts can spearhead professional development for their colleagues by mentoring, teaching in-service classes and modeling practice.*

8. What possible challenges might your actions create and what are some ways that you could manage these challenges?
Challenges:

- *Because 100% of the staff is rated effective or highly effective there is likely to be some resistance to change when asking teachers to adjust their instruction for minority subgroups. "Why should I change, I'm rated effective/highly effective. I must be doing something right."*
- *A challenge will arise in training specific teachers with Masters' Degrees+30 credits. Highly experienced teachers might believe they've been adequately trained.*

Management:

- *In changing the culture, Mr. Susino has to understand that it is first necessary to break down barriers blocking change. By working with small groups of teachers and initiating a collegial support system, the change process could be widely accepted.*

India Expeditionary Learning Secondary School

Selected Response:
1. D
2. B
3. C
4. D

Performance Task:

1. What are two primary issues presented in this scenario, and why do you believe this to be so?

Primary issues:

- High percentage of SWDs underperforming, grades 6-11.
- Low performance at Level 3+4 for subgroups on English Language Arts, and Mathematics assessments, grades 6, 7, and 8.
- Low performance at 85% and above for all subgroups on all Regents examinations.
- Not making Adequate Yearly Progress in Science for the All Students subgroup and students receiving Free/Reduced Lunch.
- Staffing issues: 37% of teachers have three or less years' experience; 11% of teachers rated developing or ineffective.

Explanation: Inexperienced staff and underperforming subgroups are reflective of a mismatch between teaching and learning. Learning expeditions need to be reflective of skills and abilities needed by subgroups to be successful.

2. What are two important questions you must address in order to explore this issue? Explain why each is important to address.

Important questions:

- *What expertise do teachers have, especially in mathematics and science programs?*

Explanation: In assessing the scope of teachers' professional development background, a plan could then be developed to address areas of weakness and thereby strengthen the instructional program with targeted professional development.

- *Why is human capital an issue at the India Expeditionary Learning Secondary School?*

Explanation: With 37% of teachers with less than three years' experience, 25% of teachers determined as not highly qualified, and 11% of teachers receiving a developing or ineffective rating, human capital development should be a paramount issue for this school.

3. How will you go about getting answers to each question? What challenges might you face in getting answers to your questions?

Getting the answers to the first question:

- *In order to better understand human capital needs, a task force might be established and/or professional development committee should examine teacher preparedness, looking at teaching strengths and areas for improvement. With 13% of the staff rated highly effective, these teachers could take the point in this investigation.*

Challenge: Most certainly, resistance to examining instructional practice could cloud this effort as well as teachers' resistance to change.

Getting the answers to the second question:

- *Mr. Pope needs to consult with the superintendent or assistant superintendent as well as his colleagues to look for successful human capital practices. Concomitantly, Mr. Pope should enact the recommendations of the task force to establish pathways to develop more highly effective teachers throughout his staff.*

Challenge: Change is normally associated with resistance to change. Teachers (inexperienced, developing, and ineffective) will feel targeted and become defensive about changing their teaching practice unless resistance to change is reduced by bolstering their self-worth and contributions to the expeditionary learning process.

4. Describe one possible finding of your inquiry process and the potential action that finding would imply.

Finding:

- *As a result of task force work and/or professional development investigation, initiate a multi-pronged professional development program to support and develop teachers' subject area competencies and teaching modalities.*

Action:

- *Initiate professional development on multiple levels, including principles of differentiating instruction for newly hired teachers and teachers with developing and ineffective ratings. Use highly effective rated teachers to serve as mentors to operationalize professional development learnings.*

Juliet Middle School

Selected Response:
1. C
2. C
3. C
4. A

Performance Task:
1. Give one strength of Juliet Middle School. What evidence would you use to support this determination? What strategy might you use to enhance this strength?
Strengths:
- Low suspension rate (6%)
  Evidence: Table 2 - Student Demographics
  To enhance this strength: Something must be working regarding a lower suspension rate in a dysfunctional school; set up a committee to investigate what is working and transfer this strength school-wide to develop a positive school culture around student achievement.
- 82% of the teachers were rated effective and likewise only one teacher was rated ineffective.
  Evidence: Table 1 - Staffing
  To enhance this strength: A professional development committee including school leaders and teachers should identify incongruence between teacher performance and student achievement and develop an action plan. Since a large percentage of teachers are effective, the committee could survey the teachers to see what works and what their needs might be. These teachers should become mentors to take the lead around professional development, establishing relationships with their colleagues to facilitate change

in instructional methodologies for English Language Arts and Mathematics instruction.

2. List three areas of need for Juliet Middle School. What evidence would you use to support this determination?
Areas of need:
- *Low student achievement for all subgroups: English Language Arts, Mathematics, and Science achievement across grades 6, 7, and 8 for the All Students subgroup and minority subgroups is consistently below statewide averages over two years. Evidence: Tables 3 (a, b & c), 4 (a, b, & c), and Table 5 – English Language Arts, Mathematics , and Science Achievement*
- *Staffing issues:*
  High teacher turnover rate (42%), high percentage of teachers teaching out of license (49%), high percentage of teachers not highly qualified (40%), no teachers rated as highly effective (0%)
  Evidence: Table 1 - Staffing
- *Subgroup achievement issues:*
  34% of students are identified as Limited English Proficient; 23% of the students are classified as Students with Disabilities; low average daily attendance (88%); poverty impacted student population (91% receive free/reduced lunch)
  Evidence: Table 2 – Student Demographics

3. Which area of need would be your highest priority? Explain why.
Highest priority need:
- *Student achievement*

Explanation: Being identified as a persistently struggling school implies that students' achievement is a major issue over the past years and that improving teaching and learning is an imperative. To address these achievement struggles, teaching and learning strategies must be examined and pathways for improvement developed. Improvement implies collaborative participation of the entire school community (school leaders, teachers, parents, community organizations, and students) which has been lacking to date.

4. What are two important questions you must answer to address your highest priority? Explain why each question is important to address.
Important questions:

- *What can be done to effectively address the declining student achievement?*

Explanation: By identifying the cause for students' underachievement, the school can move from its persistently struggling status to more effectively address students' learning needs.

- *How can the school build a culture of collaboration to effectively address students' underachievement?*

Explanation: Developing human capital is crucial and should be the driving force for changing expectations and modifying practice.

5. How would you go about getting answers to each question?
Getting the answer to the first question:

- *Set up a school data committee with teachers and school leaders working collaboratively to examine the student achievement across the grades. Establish lead teacher positions by department for identified effective teachers so that they might collaboratively work with their colleagues on identifying and implementing data-driven instructional strategies to meet the needs of underachieving students.*

Getting the answer to the second question:

- *Establish a school leadership committee to examine staffing issues and student underachievement. The teacher turnover rate, the number of teachers teaching out of license, teacher ratings, and the lack of highly effective rated teachers as well as a number of teachers considered not highly qualified merits review by the school leadership committee. At the same time, consult with the superintendent or assistant superintendent to get their perspective about these issues.*

6. What actions would you take to address the school's priority need? Explain why.
Actions:

- *Establish a professional development committee including school leaders, lead teachers, and classroom teachers to investigate strategies for improving student achievement and develop a plan for professional development.*
- *Conduct staff and student surveys to identify instructional strategies that work.*
- *Conduct a series of short term and long term in-service professional development to meet the identified student achievement needs.*
- *Visit similar schools to see what works for them.*
- *Get input from the superintendent or assistant superintendent on the action plan developed.*
- *Contact local universities to see how they might be of assistance.*

Explanation: If the goal is improved student achievement, then these actions would change the school's culture from dysfunction to a collaborative learning environment.

7. How would you leverage the identified strength of the school to address the priority need?

Leveraging strength:

- *With 82% of the staff rated effective; a potential for human capital improvement exists using effective staff to lead professional development. These successful teachers need to share successful strategies that address students' achievement issues. Effective teachers could become lead teachers and guide colleagues to develop more effective teaching strategies.*

8. What possible challenges might your actions create and what are some ways that you could manage these challenges?

Action: Establish a professional development committee including school leaders, lead teachers, and classroom teachers to identify a plan for professional development.

- *Challenge: Participation in any committee can prove to be challenging; teachers may be resistant to initiating any change in practice, especially involving participation on a committee that may identify their peers as needing assistance. This could prove to be very uncomfortable.*
- *Management: Work with members of the professional development committee to understand their goal is improving teaching and student learning.*

Action: Conduct staff and student surveys to identify instructional strategies that work.

- *Challenge: Getting surveys completed by a reluctant staff could be problematic; teachers need to see the benefit of their participation.*
- *Management: Empower lead teachers to work with colleagues and students in completion of surveys. Incentivize the completion of surveys.*

Action: Conduct a series of short term and long term in-service professional development to meet the identified learning needs.

- *Challenge: Participation in professional development is always a challenge; teachers rated effective may be self-satisfied with their abilities and place blame for students' underachievement on other factors.*
- *Management: Conduct a series of workshops for teachers to shift culture from complacency to engagement. Also mandatory professional development may bring up collective bargaining issues.*

Action: Visit similar schools to see what works for them.

- *Challenge: Teachers may be reluctant to visit other schools: "their problems are not our problems."*
- *Management: Conduct visits first with lead teachers who would come back to share their positive experiences and who could re-visit those schools with their colleagues.*

Action: Get input from the superintendent or assistant superintendent on the action plan developed.

- *Challenge: The superintendent or assistant superintendent may have a different pathway for the school's improvement which may be different from the principal's vision.*
- *Management: Suggest that the superintendent or assistant superintendent visit with the school's committees and offer support (verbal or financial) for the change process.*

Action: Contact local universities to see how they might be of assistance.

- *Challenge: Identifying appropriate outside expertise. University experts might be viewed as interfering in the improvement process.*

174

- *Management: Meet with university personnel and develop an action plan for their involvement using lead teachers to model the partnership activities.*

Kilo High School

Selected Response:
1. D
2. D
3. B
4. B

Performance Task:

1. Identify one strength of the school, citing evidence to support your response.

Strengths:

- 33% of the teaching staff has a Master's Degree+30 credits.
  Evidence: Table 1 – Staffing
- 82% of the teachers have been rated Effective or Highly Effective.
  Evidence: Table 1 – Staffing
- There are no teachers "not highly qualified."
  Evidence: Table 1 – Staffing
- Low suspension rate (3%)
  Evidence: Table 2 – Student Demographics
- Moderate success in passing Regents at the 55% and 65% levels.
  Evidence: Tables 5a, 5b, 5c, and 5d – Regents Examination Results
- ELLs moved from Beginning to Advanced and Proficient after two years
  Evidence: Table 6 – New York State English as a Second Language Achievement
- The All Students subgroup achieved AYP in English Language Arts and Overall Graduation Rate
  Evidence: Tables 7 and 8 - Accountability

2. *Identify three areas of need in the instructional program, citing evidence to support each need.*
Areas of need:

- *Graduation rate – Only 79% of students graduating received a Regents diploma. (State guidelines require 80%).*
  Evidence: Table 3 - High School Completers
- *Low aspirations of graduates – None of the high school completers went to four year colleges.*
  Evidence: Table 4 - Post-Graduation Plans of Completers
- *Academic performance: There are very small numbers of students who performed at the 85% level and above on Regents examinations. Additionally subgroups underperformed on State examinations in English Language Arts and Mathematics.*
  Evidence: Table 5a, 5b, 5c, and 5d - Regents Examination Results
- *Accountability – AYP in English Language Arts not achieved for Black and Free/Reduced Lunch subgroups. AYP in Mathematics not achieved for the All Students subgroup, Black and Free/Reduced Lunch subgroups. AYP for graduation not achieved for SWDs.*
  Evidence: Tables 7 and 8 - Accountability and Graduation Rate Accountability

3. *Which area of need would be your highest priority? Explain why.*
High priority need:

- *The highest priority need is better achievement on Regents examinations.*
  Explanation: If student achievement improved across subgroups, then the graduation rate would improve, students' success would be enhanced and Adequate

Yearly Progress would be attained for all subgroups. Concomitantly a greater rate for admission to four year colleges would result.

4. What are two important questions you must answer to address your highest priority? Explain why each question is important to address.
Important questions:
- *Why are students not performing at higher levels on State assessments and Regents examinations?*

Explanation: Improving student achievement implies developing a culture that facilitates change. There is a disconnect between staff expertise and teacher preparation to teach underachieving subgroups.

- *Why is there a disconnect between staff effectiveness (APPR) and teacher preparation?*

Explanation: 82% of teachers are rated either effective or highly effective, yet the school has been identified as persistently struggling. The teachers' expertise is not in alignment with their students' achievement.

5. How will you go about getting answers to each question?
Getting the answer to the first question:
- *Establish a data committee to examine achievement data, looking for disconnects between student achievement and teaching preparation. The committee could look at other schools' performance to see how similar schools performed and how their success could be transferrable to Kilo High School. The principal should consult with the superintendent or assistant superintendent to review teacher performance criteria. The principal should enlist the assistance of a local university/college to support looking at student achievement and instructional methodologies.*

Getting the answer to the second question:

- *The data committee should look for any disconnect between curriculum, instruction, and assessment. The committee should look at teachers' practice to see if it meets students' needs. Survey the teachers to see their perceptions of preparedness to teach these subgroups. Consult with superintendent or assistant superintendent to review teacher evaluations to see if they were aligned with student achievement and state assessments.*

6. What actions would you take to address the school's priority need? Explain why.
Actions:

- *Establish a data team to evaluate student achievement looking for disconnects between Regents performance and the taught curriculum.*
- *Work collaboratively with identified teachers whose work with students' Regents performance is exemplary to lead an initiative to improve teaching and learning across their departments.*
- *Identify Regents successful experienced teachers to provide professional development to their colleagues.*
- *Conduct visits with Kilo teachers to other similar high schools whose Regents performance is exemplary to see what works and could be transported back to Kilo High School.*

Explanation: All these actions require greater participation and collaboration of teachers. In order to facilitate change and improve teaching and learning, a shift in cultural expectations must occur. By identifying a cadre of Regents successful teachers, a core group is now available to begin facilitating change. Professional learning communities could be established to initiate collaborative work for improving Regents performance.

7. How would you leverage the identified strength of the school to address the priority need?
Strengths: 33% of the teaching staff has a master's degree+30 credits; 82% of the teachers have been rated Effective or Highly Effective; there are no teachers "not highly qualified."
Leveraging strengths:
- *With an experienced staff, use their expertise to lead efforts in school reform by identifying and training a cadre of teachers that could lead this effort working collaboratively with their peers to modify curricular experiences that meets their students' needs, and spearhead professional development.*

8. What possible challenges might your actions create and what are some ways that you could manage these challenges?
Action: Establish a data team to evaluate student achievement looking for disconnects between Regents performance and the taught curriculum.
- *Challenge: Posting the advertisement with specific criteria for committee participation would eliminate the challenge of having teachers with less than exemplary Regents performance wanting to participate in this process. Also when identified, committee members must be cognizant of their confidentiality in looking at student and teacher performance.*
- *Management: The data committee requires training in looking at a variety of data for both students and teachers Additionally, training in how to be confidential in their work and how to work collaboratively with their peers is also required.*

180

Action: Work collaboratively with identified teachers whose work with students' Regents performance is exemplary to lead an initiative to improve teaching and learning across their departments.

- *Challenge: Identifying exemplary teachers would definitely be challenging since a large number of teachers have been rated as effective or highly effective. Likewise, initiating a program to move teachers out of their comfort zone to modify teaching and learning for colleagues could also prove to be challenging.*
- *Management: This challenge could be managed by developing a job description, advertising the position, and setting up a committee to interview candidates. The committee must select well respected high performing teachers with the ability to influence their peers.*

Action: Identify Regents successful experienced teachers to provide professional development to their colleagues.

- *Challenge: Identifying teachers that have the appropriate skills to conduct professional development could be challenging, since a large number of teachers have been rated effective or highly effective.*
- *Management: This challenge could be managed by developing a job description, requiring the unique skills and abilities required to be a lead teacher. Upon advertising the position, the data committee would interview candidates knowing the qualities of lead teachers beforehand.*

Action: Conduct visits with Kilo teachers to other similar high schools whose Regents performance is exemplary to see what works and could be transported back to Kilo High School.

- *Challenge: Identify similar high performing high schools that have addressed student achievement issues and staff preparedness and whose Regents performance is beyond expectation.*
- *Management: Teachers from identified schools and teachers from Kilo High School could collaborate about teaching underperforming students that Kilo teachers could bring back to Kilo High School.*

The Lima Preparatory School

Selected Response:

1. A
2. B
3. C
4. D

Performance Task:

1. What are two primary issues presented by the data and why do you believe it to be so?

Primary issues:

- Consistent underachievement in English Language Arts and Mathematics, grades 3-8.
- Not making Adequate Yearly Progress in English Language Arts, Mathematics, and Science.
- Most teachers are rated effective or highly effective while student achievement is abysmal.
- Student suspensions are extremely high.

Explanation: Low student achievement as evidenced in Tables 3 and 7 are indicative of a disconnect with teacher performance (Table 1). In order to improve student achievement, teachers' abilities to deliver appropriate instruction must be supported. Likewise, students are acting out most likely because of ineffective instructional strategies.

2. What are two important questions you must address as principal to explore this issue? Explain why each question is important?

Important questions:

- Why is student achievement low?

Explanation: There may be a disconnect between teaching and learning for underachieving subgroups which must be addressed to improve students' *achievement. At the same time, professional development for teachers is lacking so that instructional practice is inconsistent.*

- *Why is teachers' performance highly rated?*

Explanation: Examining this issue could lead to the development of appropriate plan of action for teachers to develop instructional strategies to meet the achievement needs of their students. The questions arise: How are the teachers evaluated? Is there an evaluation rubric in use which is aligned with instructional expectations? There appears to be no mechanisms in place that aligns instructional expectations with evaluation criteria.

3. How will you go about getting answers to each question? What challenges might you face in getting answers to your questions?

Getting the answer to the first question:

- *The most effective way to address this question includes implementation of a data committee with teacher participation to give teachers an opportunity to examine why there was a disconnect between teaching and learning strategies.*

Challenge: Teacher participation is an issue especially since a majority of teachers were rated Highly Effective and Effective, they might be reticent to address deficiencies.

Getting the answer to the second question:

- *Involve the school leaders in looking at teacher effectiveness at their charter school and compare their evaluation process with similar charter schools to see if there was a similar disconnect. Involve the charter school management committee to investigate school leader performance, teacher evaluation, and student achievement.*

Challenge: The ability to be self-critical presents a challenge for school leaders. Another round of discontinuing personnel is not the answer to resolving issues with students' underachievement.

4. Describe one possible finding of your inquiry process and the potential action that finding would imply.
Finding:
- *There is a disconnect between teaching and learning.*
- *Student achievement is not reflected in the objectives of the teachers' evaluation system.*
- *School leaders need development of leadership skills.*

Action:
- *As a result of a school review by the charter school management committee, school leaders might look towards initiating professional development for teachers and themselves to realign teaching and learning with assessment. Likewise, school leaders should develop teacher support structures to address the negative school climate and develop strategies to re-align instruction.*

185

Appendices

Appendix A

Questions for Data Teams or Individuals

1. How do you know?

2. What do you see in the data?

3. Why did you select that data?

4. What do the data tell you about each student/groups of students?

5. Which data support or refute your beliefs?

6. What patterns do you see?

7. What have you learned about your students?

8. How does this information help you determine groupings? Instructional practices?

9. What area(s) will you focus on? Why?

10. What additional data do you need about each student in determining the course of action to take?

11. What are some possible explanations/causes for what you see?

12. What actions are you going to take?

13. What progress are you making?

14. What did you accomplish (celebrate success!)

Appendix B: Leadership Strategies that Facilitate the Use of Data	
Strategies	**What to look for**
Establishing a clear vision for the use of data	Collaboration and collegiality in establishing a vision that involves constituencies looking at a school's or district's data.
Providing supports that promote a data-driven environment	Structures in place, e.g. school management committee or school data committee that facilitates a data-driven environment.
Making data an ongoing part of the improvement process	Teachers and educational leaders work collaboratively to examine the data as part of the self-renewal process.
Creating a process or structure to analyze data	Teachers and educational leaders collaboratively examining the data; the use of lead teachers or data coaches as facilitators.
Teaching students to examine their own data	Structures are in place that facilitate students' looking at their own data and helping to determine next steps or set goals for their instruction.
Providing professional development on what the data tells you and how to use it	Structures are in place that support teachers' learning about how to use their own data to inform their instruction; lead teachers or data coaches work with teachers to show them what their data tell them and how to modify their practices.
Facilitating an organizational culture that supports data use for continuous improvement	The school or district has a culture that is supportive of teachers using their data to inform instructional practice; School leaders and teachers feel free to work with data coaches or lead teachers without recrimination about pupil performance.
Providing teacher/data coach leadership	School leaders have in place lead teachers and/or data coaches to work with teachers and school based committees regarding their data and its importance to the teaching, learning and assessment processes.

Appendix C

Scenarios:	Leadership Standards									
	1. Mission, Vision, & Values	2. Ethics & Professional Norms	3. Equity & Cultural Responsiveness	4. Curriculum, Instruction & Assessment	5. Community of Care & Support for Students	6. Professional Capacity of School Personnel	7. Professional Community for Teachers and Staff	8. Meaningful Engagement of Families and Community	9. Operations and Management	10. School Improvement
1	X	X		X	X	X	X		X	X
2	X	X	X	X		X	X		X	X
3	X	X		X		X	X		X	X
4	X	X	X	X			X		X	X
5	X	X	X	X	X	X	X		X	X
6	X	X	X	X	X		X	X	X	X
7	X	X	X	X	X	X	X	X	X	X
8	X	X		X		X	X		X	X
9	X	X		X		X	X	X	X	X
10	X	X	X	X	X	X	X	X	X	X
11	X	X		X		X	X		X	X
12	X			X					X	X

189

References

Abbott, C.J., & McKnight, K (2010). Developing instructional leadership through collaborative learning. AASA Journal of Scholarship & Practice, 7(2), 20-26.
Retrieved from
http://pearsonlt.com/sites/all/files/lt/AASA%20JSP%20Abbott%20%20McKnight%202010%207-pages.pdf

American Association of School Administrators (AASA). (2002). Using data to improve schools: What's working. Arlington, VA: Author.

Bernhardt, V. L. (2005). Data Tools for School Improvement. *Educational Leadership*, *62*(5), 66.

Bernhardt, V. L. (2009). Data Use: Data-Driven Decision-making Takes a Big-Picture View of the Needs of Teachers and Students. *Journal of Staff Development*, *30*(1), 24-27.

Bernhardt, V. L. (2015). Toward Systemwide Change. *Educational Leadership, 73*(3), 56-61.

Boudett, K., Murnane, R. J., & City, E. (2005). Teaching Educators How to Use Student Assessment Data To Improve Instruction. *Phi Delta Kappan*, *86*(9), 700-706.

Carlson, D., Borman, G. D., & Robinson, M. (2011). A multi-state district-level cluster randomized trial of the impact of data-driven reform on reading and mathematics achievement. Educational Evaluation and Policy Analysis 33(3), 378398.

Chappuis, S., Chappuis, J., & Stiggins, R. (2009). The Quest for Quality. *Educational Leadership, 67*(3), 14-19.

Creighton, T. B. (2001). Data Analysis and the Principalship. Principal Leadership, 9(1), 52-57.
Retrieved from
http://www.nassp.org/portals/0/content/48166.pdf

Datnow, A., Park, V. & Wohlstetter, P. (2007). Achieving with data: How high performing Districts use data to improve instruction for elementary school students. Los Angeles,CA: Center on Educational Governance, USC Rossier School of Education.
Retrieved from
http://www.usc.edu/dept/education/cegov/focus/educati onreform/publications/books/chapters/Achieving%20wit h%20DataHow%20High%20Performing%20Schools%20Us e%20Data%5B1%5D.pdf

Datnow, A., & Park, V. (2014) <u>Data-Driven Leadership</u>. San Francisco, CA: Jossey-Bass.

Deeb-Westervelt, W., & Thompson, E. (2010). <u>Data talk: Creating teacher and administrator partnerships around data</u>. Deer Park, New York: Linus Publications.

DuFour, R. (2002). The Learning-Centered Principal. *Educational Leadership, 59*(8), 12-15.

Elmore, R. F. (2005). Accountable Leadership. Essays. *The Educational Forum, 69*(2), 134-142.

Fuglei, M. (2014). How teachers can use student data to improve instruction.
Retrieved from

http://education.cu-portland.edu/blog/news/how-teachers-use-student-data-to-improve-instruction/

Halverson, R., Grigg, J., Prichett, R., & Thomas, C. (2007). The New Instructional Leadership: Creating Data-Driven Instructional Systems in School. *Journal of School Leadership, 17*(2), 159-194.

Halverson, R. (2010). School Formative Feedback Systems. *Peabody Journal of Education, 85*(2), 130-146.

Hamilton, L., Halverson, R., Jackson, S. S., Mandinach, E., Supovitz, J. A., Wayman, J. C., What Works Clearinghouse, (2009). Using Student Achievement Data to Support Instructional Decision-making. IES Practice Guide. NCEE 2009-4067. *National Center For Education Evaluation And Regional Assistance*.

Hattie, J. (2015). The effective use of testing: What the research says. *Education Week, 35*(10), 23 & 28.

Heritage, M., & Yeagley, R. (2005). Data Use and School Improvement: Challenges and Prospects. *Yearbook Of The National Society For The Study Of Education, 104*(2), 320-339.

Ikemoto, G., & Marsh, J. (2007). chapter 5 Cutting Through the "Data-Driven" Mantra: Different Conceptions of Data-Driven Decision-making. *Yearbook Of The National Society For The Study Of Education (Wiley-Blackwell), 106*(1), 105-131.

Kazemi, E. & Franke, M. L. (2003). Using student work to support professional development in elementary mathematics. Seattle, WA: University of Washington, Center for the Study of Teaching and Policy.

Retrieved from
https://depts.washington.edu/ctpmail/PDFs/Math-EKMLF-04-2003.pdf

Kennedy, B. L., & Datnow, A. (2011). Student Involvement and Data-Driven Decision-making: Developing a New Typology. *Youth & Society, 43*(4), 1246-1271.

Lachat, M.A. & Smith, S. (2005). Practices that support data use in urban high schools. Journal of Education for Students Placed at Risk, 10, 333-349.

Leahy, S., Lyon, C., Thompson, M., & William, D. (2005). Classroom Assessment: Minute by Minute, Day by Day. *Educational Leadership, 63*(3), 18-24.

Leithwood, K., Louis, K., Anderson, S., & Wahlstrom, K. (2004). How leadership influences student learning. New York, NY: Wallace Foundation.
Retrieved from
http://www.wallacefoundation.org/knowledge-center/school-leadership/key-research/Documents/How-Leadership-Influences-Student-Learning.pdf

Mandinach, E. B., Honey, M., & Light, D. (2006). A theoretical framework for data-driven decision-making. American Educational Research Association, San Francisco, CA.
Retrieved from
http://cct.edc.org/sites/cct.edc.org/files/publications/DataFrame_AERA06.pdf

Mandinach, E. B. (2012). A Perfect Time for Data Use: Using Data-Driven Decision-making to Inform Practice. *Educational Psychologist, 47*(2), 71-85.

Marsh, J. A., Pane, J. F. & Hamilton, L. S. (2006). Making sense of data-driven decision-making in education. Retrieved from
http://www.rand.org/content/dam/rand/pubs/occasional papers/2006/RAND OP170.pdf

Marsh, J. A., Bertrand, M., & Huguet, A. (2015). Using data to alter instructional practice: The mediating role of coaches and professional learning communities. *Teachers College Record*, 117 (4), 1-40.

McAdamis, S. (2007). A View of the Future: Teamwork Is Daily Work. *Journal of Staff Development*, 28(3), 43.

McIntire, T. (2005). Data: Maximize your mining, Part One. Teach Learning. Retrieved from
http://www.techlearning.com/assessment-&-testing/0034/data-maximize-your-mining-part-one/45194

McQuiggan, J., & Sapp III, A. W. (2014). Lessons for a data culture: Adapted from Implement, improve and expand your statewide longitudinal data system: Creating a culture of data in education.

National Policy Board for Educational Administration (2015). Professional Standards for Educational Leaders 2015. Reston, VA.

New York State Public Data Access Site, New York State Education Department, 2015.
All data for charts and graphs were obtained from the public access website.
http://data.nysed.gov/lists.php?type=school

New York State Teacher Certification Examinations, Pearson, Inc. (2016) School Building Leader Examination Test Preparation Questions
Retrieved from:
http://www.nystce.nesinc.com/NY_PM.asp?t=107

Oberman, I., Arbeit, C., Praglin, C., Goldsteen, S. (2005). Challenged schools, remarkable results: Three lessons from California's highest achieving high schools. San Francisco, CA: Springboard Schools.
Retrieved from
http://www.issuelab.org/resource/challenged_schools_re markable_results_three_lessons_from_California's_ highest_achieving_high_schools

Schmoker, M. (2004). Tipping Point: From Feckless Reform to Substantive Instructional Improvement. *Phi Delta Kappan, 85*(6), 424-432.

Smith, R., Johnson, M., & Thompson, K. D. (2012). Data, Our GPS. *Educational Leadership, 69*(5), 56-59.

Sternke, J. (2016). Answering the question: "How do you know?" *School Administrator (February 2016)*, 34-36.

Stiggins, R., & Chappuis, J. (2006). What a Difference a Word Makes: Assessment "for" Learning Rather than Assessment "of" Learning Helps Students Succeed. *Journal of Staff Development, 27*(1), 10-14.

Tomlinson, Carol Ann (2015). Different Data, Different Roles. *Educational Leadership, 73*(3), 87-88.

Valli, L., & Buese, D. (2007). The Changing Roles of Teachers in an Era of High-Stakes Accountability. *American Educational Research Journal, 44*(3), 519-558.

Wayman, J. C., & Stringfield, S. (2006). Leadership for data-based decision-making: Collaborative data teams. American Educational Research Association, San Francisco CA.
Retrieved from http://edadmin.edb.utexas.edu/datause/papers/Wayman-Midgley-Stringfield-AERA2006.pdf

Wayman, J., Cho, V., Jimerson, J., & Spikes, D. (2012). District-Wide Effects on Data Use in the Classroom. *Education Policy Analysis Archives*, *20*(25), 1-27.

We have established an email account to answer reasonable questions about using data as educational leaders.

diving.into.data@gmail.com

If you have questions and/or comments about selected response questions or performance tasks, kindly email us. We will respond!